LOVING
THE ME IN ME

GROUNDING IN
THE LOVE VIBRATION

FRANCES PULLIN

Loving the Me in Me
Grounding in the Love Vibration

Copyright © 2018 by Frances Pullin

Editor: Roni Askey-Doran
Interior Design: Jera Publishing
Cover Design: Jera Publishing

First Edition

ISBN   978-0-9903932-3-8 (print)
        978-0-9903932-4-5 (eBook)

ACKNOWLEDGMENT

This book became a reality after meeting a fabulously inspirational woman, Roni Askey-Doran. We met through a writer's group on Facebook. Talking back and forth, and supporting each other, we became caring friends. When I spoke to her about Amadeus' message asking me to consider looking into the mirror and learn to love me, and to then teach love of self to children, she told me her story. She, too, had been asked to look in the mirror and, at the time, the thought had petrified her. But, she did it! She did it and, after a long year or more of hard work, she learned to love herself. Currently, Roni's laughter is spontaneous and her humor contagious as she traverses through life.

I met Roni in the flesh in Los Angeles when she flew in from her seaside dwelling in a fishing village in South America for the book signing of her novel, *Broken*. We chatted like old friends, and another woman from our book club helped her with makeup and wardrobe for the big day. We lunched and enjoyed the way the Universe had brought us all together, hearing tales of her adventures around the world.

What stuck in my mind was the realness of this woman whose life had been riddled with mishaps and misadventures which had caused her to fall out of love of her. When we met, I was seeing the result of the work she had put into changing her life into a beautiful story of giving and caring for the Earth, the animals and the people. She had turned her turmoil into some sense of order. She loved the person she was. You might want to read her book, *I'm Bipolar and I Know It*. She spent much of her life finding love of self.

It is with her story I knew I could rewrite mine. I have written on the pages of this book, my story of unloved to loved. You can too. We all can.

DEDICATION

I dedicate this book to my parents who loved me all the time, even when I didn't recognize it. They did the best they could to bring order to my existence. I chose them for the lessons which will be revealed in this missive.

CONTENTS

FOREWORD

By: Michelle Montagno

I was surprised and deeply flattered when my mother asked me to write the foreword in her new book. I had to take some time to think about what I wanted to say. As the oldest of her children, I feel like we grew up together in some ways. As a mother myself, I know how difficult it can be. I look back and see the young girl who was trying to be a good Mom yet making oh so many mistakes. We are so hard on ourselves and so sure people will discover how terrible we are at being human. We aren't, of course, but it feels like every mistake is huge. This book, at its heart, is about love of self. It always sounds like such a simple concept, and yet, it is the one most people have trouble with. The death of my brother Damon set my mother on this incredible path of spirituality and enlightenment. I think while she was looking for ways to communicate with him, and understand the why of it all, she discovered her true self. It's been amazing to watch her journey and, ultimately, I believe she is sharing it with all of you so that you might find the love of you in you.

INTRODUCTION

What would it take to love the 'you' in you? What would it take for you to begin to recognize you have a place in the restoring of the health of the Earth? Love of self turns into love of others and perpetuates a therapy known to few who exist in this lifetime. Have you ever really thought about it? Most of us have not. Mother Theresa, Gandhi, and the Dali Lama, perhaps have, but what about us, regular folks? Is it something the masses think about? What about those beginning their spiritual journey, knowing there is so much to discover about helping others, healing them, and moving into grace and love in this lifetime? We know we should love others, but what about the 'me' in me, and the 'you' in you?

The message of this book stems from an infinite lack of love. It is a world-wide issue. There doesn't seem to be enough of it flowing through the minds and hearts of the multitudes on the earth plane. Do you listen to what is going on in this world of untold beauty? There is destruction, starvation and mayhem.

The time has come to learn about the vibration that we have forgotten and bring an end to the uncertainty of not loving you. It masks the beauty I speak about.

Perhaps you have never stopped to think about it as you rush about trying to exist in your busy lives. You are not alone. There are countless souls who have no idea what to do with the ills of the world, yet famine, fear, destruction and killing surround the existence of many. Perhaps you have ideas and don't know of a way to bring your solutions to the masses. Hopefully you will be better equipped to bring these resolutions to the world after learning to love you.

Through this book, as we learn love of self, we will begin to heal these atrocities. Until recently, this devastation may have gone unnoticed, but with the constant reports of bombings, killings and mayhem being broadcast from every television, radio, newspaper, and through social media, we can no longer ignore the truth of what the world is going through. Placing no judgment on your journey, I ask you to take a moment to think about all souls in the world currently in crisis, lacking love of self and others.

"Crazy old woman, what do you mean love the 'you' in you?" you question. Where would that thought have come from? It certainly isn't part of most people's world. Yes, there are the vain, the boasters, the arrogant. They don't truly love themselves. They are mostly insecure. I am talking about the true love of self. Yes, I love the 'me' in me. This is something I had to learn how to do and I wish to share it with you. Self-love can be so powerful that it can bring an entire world together in peace and untold joy. It can move your energy to a place of beauty, harmony, and tranquility. Have you looked for it? Have you found it? Have you felt it? I will take you on a journey to demonstrate this profound love and assist you in learning how to create this feeling inside of you.

So, it begins. During meditation this morning, January 16, 2015, I was directed by my family and friends in the Spirit World to write with them, along with my Guides, Angels and Elementals, my Team. They are all in harmony over this project. It appears my son, Damon (who suddenly departed the Earth in 2003), oversees the project. He is allowing all on the Other Side to help.

"I am having trouble getting started. I don't know what to write about. I know you all want a book, but how do I develop it?"

Greetings, Lovely Lady,

We were all with you last night and know you felt our presence. You will sit at the keyboard as directed before and the tale will unfold. You are a strong, heartfelt woman with many stories in this lifetime. Pull from past lives also. Your style has been created and, so it is that we will be co-creating the book. Damon has been put in charge to lead us through a beautiful story and conclusion. Your Mom and Dad are with you also. We are jubilant with the reconciliation of your parents and yourself. Go, create, and publish. We have brought to you a place in time for you to chronicle your life in this new venue.

Loving the Me in Me

> **Keep arranging your words on paper and it will
> be a true, factual, healing force. Go now, begin.
> You've not a moment to lose!**
>
> **Love, Us**

CHAPTER 1

My Youth

I grew up in a family of seven children. Yes, seven. I was born on May 23, 1949 in Los Alamos, New Mexico, in the USA, to be exact. Large families sprouted up all over the country as soldiers returned from WWII to the spouses and girlfriends who had waited for them. It is an era known to the world as the Baby Boom! The explosion of gunfire was silenced and replaced with new souls who came squalling into the world for yet another life on Earth. Birth control was practiced by few. Some did not practice for religious reasons and some just because it was cumbersome.

How do you love seven children equally? The fact is, you don't. How can you? Some are easy, and some are not. We had all shapes and sizes. There was the oldest, the rebel, the good child, the sickly one, the naughty one, the quiet one, the baby.

Some demanded to be heard and tended to. I was one who tried to quietly meld into the background, hoping to be overlooked by being obedient.

With all our needs, how could my parents stay on top of the chaos? Chaos is the best way to describe the household I grew up in. There, third out of seven, I became the 'good' child. I got decent grades, and participated in school activities, I hunkered down in my room whenever possible with an enjoyable biography or autobiography borrowed from the Book Mobile that visited our neighborhood shopping center once a month. It was in this same room that my mother admonished me for having my nose stuck in another book and not being part of the family. I was accused of thinking I was better than the rest of them when I was just hiding. Not that I knew it at that time, but that's what I was doing. I wandered the world through words on paper that were bound together with love. I avoided any interaction that might contribute to the use of the belt on my back, legs or behind. I avoided being a part of the screaming and criticism. Alas, even by disappearing into my room, I was found out and critiqued with disdain anyway.

So, by staying out of the way as much as possible, I never asked to be loved. I didn't know what it was or what I was missing, so I never demanded it. I was told once as a child, by my mother, that I was loved. At least, it's the only time I can remember those words. The scene has stuck with me throughout this lifetime. After a few whacks on my backside with whatever was in her hand at that moment, she was saddened by what she had done. She told me she had to hit me because she loved me; because I needed to behave, and it was her job to teach me. Yes, that is the memory. That was a time I subconsciously began to realize I wasn't worthy of her love. That I was somehow bad. I didn't comprehend the notion of being unloved at that sensitive time, but it began to become a part of who I was.

As for my father, I don't remember ever hearing words of love from him. He was a tough disciplinarian. No nonsense was usually the tone he exuded, and we dreaded his arrival home from work. Who knew how his day or night had been, or who needed to run for cover. Sometimes, on a seemingly ordinary day, each one of us could become the target.

Love was not a priority to many families in that era. They were just trying to hang on to their own souls. Those who had returned from war were trying to process the destruction they had seen and played a part in. Not wishing to be a part of the war but seeing it as their duty to defend their country and honor the mandatory draft for young men which was in effect, many joined up before being drafted so they could choose which branch of the military they wished to spend their time with.

Seven children, a wife and a high-stress career haunted my father's days and nights. He was an Air Traffic Controller who worked a different shift each week. He wasn't equipped with the appropriate coping mechanisms to withstand the pressures of the seven squabbling children, six of which he had created and brought into the world. (My oldest sister was the child of my mother and her first husband.) Regularly, he exploded. Once the rage subsided, an eerie silence fell upon the household. Many cried softly so as not to be hit again.

Yes, I know why it happened. I have found a way to forgive him. Once I married and left the house, he became a friend to turn to. We have chatted at length since his passing. I realize how ridiculous that sounds to those of you who do not yet understand how it's possible to communicate with those on the Other Side. But, I have experienced many moments where we were able to forgive each other; me for my conceived imperfections, and he for his.

I was not always hiding in the shadows. Sometimes, I was out later at night than was allowed and the 'good' child caused worry for both of my parents. Was this their way of loving me? By controlling me? The punishment from that ever-looming belt being pulled from its loops didn't feel remotely like love. The welts I wore to school for days afterwards did not compel me to come home. I rejoiced while I was outside of the energy of the place I called home, feeling like a free bird surrounded by laughter and merriment.

There was the rare occasion, though, when you could find my dad playing jacks with my sisters and me on the front porch. Was that love? I imagine when I think about it now, it was a form of peace, if not love itself. It was pleasant enough. During those times of frivolity, I didn't feel aversion or fear.

Our summer vacations were usually camping trips to the mountains around Sedona, Arizona. As a child, I did not know that the energy vortexes found in that area could bring a sense of peace to this tribe. I only knew we were in a semi-public place and things seemed to operate on a more even keel. Once the barrage of cursing that helped raise the tent was over, everything else was put smoothly into place. The best smell in my life is still the first whiff of the fire in the chilly morning air. Dad built the fire while we were snuggled in our sleeping bags, waiting to be summoned to the picnic table for our breakfast. It was where we all escaped our realities and came together in peace and harmony. The energy in the area around Sedona unknowingly brought balance to all our energies.

Love was, I imagine, to be snagged out of thin air any time a parent took any notice of one of us. Negative or positive attention brought with it a feeling that we were cared for, in some vague way. I never remember even thinking about whether I was loved or not. I just found my place in the hierarchy.

Do you remember being hugged as a child? I rarely remember feeling blessed with that exchange of love energy I have since come to know as an adult. That was not what we did. Where in the day or night would there be time to pass out hugs to seven children? The caring of the babies, cleaning, laundry, and cooking took a toll on my mother. This was a time with wringer washers, outdoor laundry lines, ironing the clothes. Those baby diapers were washed, hung to dry and folded every few days. No paper diapers to be tossed in the trash and subsequently buried in a landfill. There wasn't a microwave to speed up the meal preparation process and my father demanded meat, potatoes, vegetable, salad and bread at each meal, and on Sundays, dessert. No frozen prepackaged meals were at anyone's table back then. My mother looked forward to the time she could teach us those tasks, so her life would become a little easier. A tidy household was not her aspiration. My father disagreed. She was raised in squalor and him in impeccable surroundings. I am sure the disarray of our home added to his ire.

As early as four years old, I learned how to do the dishes. One sister washed, one rinsed, one dried and my mother put them away. We were too short in stature to reach the cupboards, so she placed tubs of wash and rinse water on chairs in front of the sink, so we could tackle the job demanded of us. Once we could conquer the chores, she was able to escape to the neighbor's house for coffee, cigarettes and gossip. Life in the suburbs was hers, if only for a few hours.

Dad has explained to me, in his spirit form, that neither of my parents were raised with the love I am eluding to here. They each had tough childhoods. My father's father crossed over when my dad was eleven, struck by a drunken driver as he ended his shift at the trolley station. My grandfather was found lying in the street mangled and already gone. The car that had struck him was located near the scene and the driver confessed to the deed.

Within six months, my father's brother also left the Earth, drowning in the local lake. It was another tragic accident affecting the hearts of the entire family. Soon thereafter, his mother, my grandmother, was diagnosed with cancer. My father, then twelve, and his two sisters were sent to live with an aunt in Nebraska. In those days, cancer was hushed away and treated as a contagious disease. She recovered and moved to Nebraska to reunite with the children.

The family, without a father as the bread winner, suffered from the lack of money. My dad worked odd jobs to add to the funds his mother earned, but there was just not enough to feed the two remaining siblings and his mother. Alas, my father joined the Civilian Conservation Corps at aged fifteen, and never returned home to his mother's knee. The family needed support following the depression, and he was looking for a way to help take care of his mother and two sisters. Without a proper education or any working skills, Roosevelt's job program was his only viable option. As much of his paycheck as possible was sent home to his family.

Dad enlisted in the Army at the impressionable age of seventeen, lying about his age, and subsequently went off to war; he was still a child. World War II had erupted, and all healthy young men were suited up and sent across the oceans to defend their country. He was stationed in Guam and was a radio controller hassled endlessly by the group known as "Tokyo Rose." Because of Tokyo Rose and their evil way of manipulating allied troops about being taken over by the enemy, the propaganda drove him to madness. He blacked out, and was shipped to Hawaii housed in a cage, deep in the bowels of a great ship. It was there, in Hawaii, where he was finally treated. He had lost an entire thirty days of his life. Today they would call his condition Post Traumatic Stress Disorder, but at that time there was no such diagnosis, so he was treated for depression. My father was prescribed medication to stabilize his behavior and keep his mind at peace.

At times, as I was growing up, after a particularly stupendous row between my parents, my mother would drag out the tired old subject of his meds as though it was a dirty little secret. She was a tiny woman and he was a big strong man, and this was her only control. It was all she had. In that day, mental illness was swept under the rug and rarely talked about. As a teenager and young adult, I finally made sense of her angry whispering to him and slamming the bottle of pills on the counter. Years later, after hearing vague stories of his war experiences, it became clear that his outbursts became uncontrollable if he failed to medicate himself.

My mother was born on a farm in North Dakota. For a time, she lived in a railway boxcar alongside many of her cousins, aunts and uncles, her seven siblings and parents. The family farm had failed during the Great Depression of the 30's and 40's and was repossessed.

Apparently, there was no time for loving hugs or goodnight kisses as this family struggled to stay alive. Mom left home at eighteen to work at Boeing in Seattle. While living there, she married a man she met in the city. While she was still pregnant with her first child, they divorced. Her husband found his pending responsibility daunting and wanted out of the predicament he'd put himself in.

She was living in Seattle where she was raising her baby daughter when she met my father, who was one of her brother's Army buddies. The two men had met while serving together in the war. Two months later, my Mom and Dad were married. At the young age of twenty-two, they were in it for life. For richer, for poorer, in sickness and in health, they remained married until my Dad's passing at age sixty-eight, twenty-seven years ago.

This brings me to pause for a moment, at my own young age of sixty-eight, knowing his life had been cut short by lung cancer. Was this the hand Karma had dealt him for being who he was in this lifetime, or maybe another? Was it a way for him to move on from a very difficult lesson after having learned that lesson? Perhaps it was—his children were on their own and, after retirement, he was often bored and felt alone. The man we were so frightened of had softened and became very caring of his grandchildren and his children. The pressures of raising his brood had been released and the true caring giant emerged.

My father told me his previous generation taught that hugging, saying "I love you", and praise only served to raise a spoiled brat. We were brought up to be strong and, for the most part, we are. My siblings (the ones I speak to on a regular basis) do not end a telephone conversation without an "I love you." We don't leave each other's energy without a warm hug. We taught this affectionate habit to each other as we grew within our own individual lives and subsequent families.

What my parents gave us materially was so much more than they had been raised with. They had learned to provide for their family financially, just not how to show love. They felt adjunct pride in the fact that they owned a home in the suburbs of Tucson, Arizona and could clothe and feed seven children. We didn't have the frills of owning special party dresses or pastel colored Capezio slippers, but we were never hungry. The thought that there might be anything missing in their children's lives never entered my parent's minds. I won't dwell on this history any longer. It was what I was part of, and a portion of the lessons I needed to learn and understand while I was here on the Earth in this incarnation. I learned them well.

Discovering how to express my love to my own children, to kiss them, hug them and read them stories seemed to come so naturally. After all, I had observed this unfamiliar hugging behavior among my school mates and I wanted to be part of it! I had seen my friends receiving hugs and kisses from their parents and each other. That was the time in my life when I first began to demonstrate physical affection. A hug with a friend. So simple, yet also awkward. I had to teach myself how to relax, to give and receive that much longed-for exchange. The importance of human contact via the warmth of holding hands or a hug given and received has been documented by health practitioners the world over. Many years later, I recognized this was the first lesson in learning to love the 'me' in me. I had begun grounding in the love vibration. Slowly but surely, I began to feel love. Perhaps I had known this exchange in a past lifetime. I may investigate that one day.

It is I, Amadeus, Sweet One.

Good morning to you. It is delightful to sit with you and hear the story of your parents and the effect they had upon your life in this lifetime. Already knowing how it unfolded, we are now aware of how it was seen through your eyes. You have been with them before, but the lessons are new and there have been many.

You have chosen your siblings in the same way you chose your parents and the children that have come into your life. The lessons you learned in the family home at the knee, so to speak, of your mother and father have sometimes been difficult and yet so necessary to bring you to the place you revel in at this time of your life.

Do not dwell on the issues that you write about. You are writing them to tell the story of Frances in this lifetime and you have forgiven all the issues and healed all the bonds between yourself and your parents. They are standing by and allowing their faults to be shown so the story resonates with your audience.

It is beautiful to see the words flow and the story to reveal itself knowing that the outcome will be at the end of this manuscript when we are certain you have attained the love of self that you so desire. Remember, Dear One, it is just a story.

Go in love and light, Amadeus.

CHAPTER II

Fast Forward

oth of my parents have passed on. I receive messages from them during public and private mediumship sessions, and after my personal meditations. During those special mediumship events I have attended, a medium brings forth the energy of a spirit who reveals themselves to him/her. The room is full of spirits. They have been called by the spectators who seek to create a connection with their loved ones. As they step forward, each spirit is described so the people in the audience can identify their loved ones either by name, stature, cause of death, or a special bond only the receiver would know. A message is passed from the deceased, through the medium, to the person in the audience who has identified them.

After personal meditation, I recognize the spirits of my family beside me, and write down the answers to any questions I ask them. It took months of study with several teachers to begin to recognize my parent's energy when they appeared. I learned what was required of me to connect with them and can now do so on a regular basis. I am keenly aware of my son, Damon, and my brother, David, who both now reside on the Other Side of the veil. They were much easier to identify because of the strong bonds I had with them, created while they walked with me in this lifetime. My son and brother have become great friends and often arrive together to chat with me. They want me to understand they have formed this deep friendship since departing, never having been close during their time together on Earth. David enjoys telling me of his love for the memories he has of us as children. I am glad he holds onto those memories. It wasn't always a great time for him. (My sister, Patricia, has also joined her parents now and I seek to find her energy one day soon. She was my protector as often as she could be during our childhood she confided a few years before her passing. She hated the way my body bruised from the beatings so would stand in for me whenever she could. I am forever grateful for that loving gesture.)

My brother did not have an easy life here on his journey on Earth. He was the most abused of all my siblings. He was challenged at every corner of his life until he found God and spirituality. There was something unusual with the way my brother connected the dots of his life. ADD, ADHD, who knows what label would be placed on this great guy in today's world.

I would have breakfast with him when I came to Tucson for a visit and listen to him talk and laugh. I miss that. I can still hear the laughter around us as I write; all the while knowing his pain of cancer was gone, his lessons learned, and his heart healed. I hope he pops in for a visit one day soon.

Imagine, my parents are now able to parent me with all the love and compassion I could have asked for when they walked along side me in this lifetime and now my brother enjoys them too. They are not at odds with each other anymore, which brings about a completeness of their journey. One of the beautiful aspects I have learned while studying spirituality is knowing that I can communicate with my family who have passed and heal the atrocities and misunderstanding of childhood.

Knowing they are all happy together brings me great joy and gives me energy and the confidence that all things are filled with love on the Other Side. Their quarreling is silenced. The pressures of life here have been replaced with a more nurturing loving atmosphere, and their souls have mended. Their journey together on this planet this time around was to bring healing to all the issues they needed to work on together. Now, they are bringing me closer to my goal of loving the 'me' in me.

At times, I wish my siblings could hear Mom and Dad's personal messages, but they choose not to venture into this awareness I refer to as Spirituality. They are on their own journeys and I cannot intervene, nor do I wish to. By interfering with their choices, I would be faulting them. There can be no negative judgement. Taking care of this soul, known as Frances, is already quite a handful according to my Master Guide, Amadeus. Admittedly, I find myself in absolute agreement.

I have done other work regarding the love between my parents and myself facilitated by Christina Gikas, a Certified Hypnotherapist here in Orange County, California. I have also participated in a current life regression for the sole purpose of correcting our misunderstanding; my parents' and mine. Christina has trained me in Hypnotherapy so that I can bring others the answers to their questions. I thank her for her guidance and friendship.

A current life regression is a session where the client is hypnotized and talked through a visit in this lifetime. I then spent time finding out and dealing with the fact that I was loved at my birth. I was always loved. I was just in a vicious cycle of frustration of my parent's volition. I visited them on the day of my birth during this session and the love they showed me at that moment in time was the information I was searching for. This piece of my life was what I was missing. I will reveal that cherished scene in a moment.

As a side note, past life regression is very much like current life regression. The client delves into a past lifetime they wish to revisit and is guided by the therapist to a specific time they wish to explore. One may be seeking to heal a certain part of this life, or possibly to understand why things are the way they are, and to figure out the exact lesson that was supposed to be learned. If this is the case, they are guided to choose the lifetime where the lesson originally began.

At times, it is to find the source of an illness or a pain in the current body. There are so many issues and lessons that can be visited through regression. I will just leave you with these brief explanations and you may seek out more information at your leisure. I have regressed both past and present lives with Christina for selected questions to be answered and will reveal more in subsequent chapters.

I am comfortable with the work that has been done. I trust my hypnotherapist with my session's confidentiality. Trust is always a key word. Trust, trust, trust. You determine what modalities are right for you to assist in your personal growth just as I have done. Smiling to myself, I realize that, even though as a writer, I have been taught not to repeat the same word in a paragraph, here it is five times. I am ignoring this rule right now as the word in question, trust, is the most important thing my Guides have ever taught me. I use it with abandon in this situation.

The session I am referring to at this moment involved my parents. I was taken subconsciously to the day I was born in this current lifetime. I envisioned my parents as they held me in their arms in the hospital room. At that moment, I was loved! It brought tears to my eyes. My mother was cradling me against her breast, beaming with the love only a mother can know.

My father reached over to bring me to his huge chest, where he too was basking in the love vibration for me, their third little girl. (As a reminder, my father had taken my oldest sister as his own. She carried his name until, at eighteen, she was allowed by law to be adopted by him.) I felt so safe in that setting. Never in my conscious life had I felt the love that had surrounded me at that moment in time.

How could that love have gotten so lost? How could either of them come to the point of striking any of their children? How did the pressure of raising children bring out such opposite emotions than those I was observing in that moment? It was for the lessons we were to learn together, and they were garnered as they were handed out during the years to come.

I was amazed by the overwhelming emotions that flooded through me as I sat, eyes closed, in the black recliner in Christina's office. Wetness trickled down my cheeks as I silently observed the gentle way my Mom and Dad caressed me and pulled back the blankets to see the ten tiny toes. Finally, I was guided to lift that precious child into my arms and breathe love into her heart.

As I hovered in that moment of time, I knew it was perfect for me to love the 'me' in me. Love of self is the greatest gift I have received in this lifetime. (Know that it did not come easily; it has taken years to achieve.) I gently presented me, the newborn, back to my mother who was glowing at her latest gift to the family. She bore such pride in her accomplishment of this loving feat, and I knew there was love in her heart, and also in my father's heart, for me.

Perfection. That is what I was at birth, and that is what I am now. It has been an arduous sixty-eight years from then until the present. Along the way, I lost that feeling of love and perfection that was shown to me as I came wailing into the hospital delivery room. It has taken a lifetime to bring me back to that vibration. I will never allow it to escape me again. I will hang onto it for lifetimes and lifetimes yet to appear. Yes, for a moment I may forget and begin to criticize myself, but there is no way I will not return to this amazingly calm feeling. I will halt the criticism and replace it with the love vibration for me.

For the first time, reclining in that chair, I recaptured the feelings of being born perfect, innocent and loved. I thank my friend, Christina, for that journey.

It is I, Amadeus, Dear One.

So, you see, in their own way, your parents loved you. You have often felt unloved. You have felt that way in other lifetimes. We are not aware when this first became a part of your energy, we

only wish for it to heal. This is one of the issues you are here to reconcile in this lifetime. You are doing a remarkable job of conquering this emotion; love of self.

You are such a sensitive soul and that never changes. Nor, do we want it to. Your sensitivity is much needed on the earth plane and on the Other Side. You bring calm resolution to all you experience. That is part of the healer in you. Healing is not always touch or sending energy through one's hands to help others heal. It is a gentle, kind listening ear filled with patience that helps many solve their issues and move forward on their path with your gentle comments.

You have always been loved but, too many times, it was not demonstrated in the way that you longed for in this incarnation. You wish to be held, rocked, cradled, hugged and kissed. You wish to hear the words, "I love you" along with these other gestures. Know that you have done this with your children and be glad. They will not have to seek this love in any lifetime as they have been rewarded it with this emotion this time. I will leave you now to return another day.

Love, Amadeus.

CHAPTER III

A People Pleaser

I am writing to you about who I am, why I am here, and what my destiny promises me. The story of me and all that I am will unfold as you turn each page in this book. The answers I seek come to me, Frances Esther Pullin, while I study, research and write with my Guides and Others after morning meditation and, at times, throughout the day. I am the unique soul, who came to the earth plane in this lifetime, who answers to that name.

I have been taught that we not only choose our family before incarnation, but also our name, birth date and time of birth. Unbelievably, we also choose the city in which we wish to be born. It defines our astrological chart which, in turn, leads us through our pre-planned destiny here on Earth.

A people pleaser. That is what I became at a very young age. It served me well over the years, but I have arrived at a time in my life where that is now changing. Realizing the love of me has directed me to take better care of myself without guilt, I have been able to change a lifelong pattern. I can now do things that lovingly best serve me without irrationally believing I am a selfish woman. The time has come for me to drop the moniker I know myself as: the people pleaser. I need to do things that please me, not others, with no harm to them or to me.

Consciously participating in activities that please me is not meant to display a self-serving attitude filled with a haughty ego, but rather serves to nurture my mind, body, spirit and soul so that I am better able to heal and care for myself and others. This is difficult, but not impossible. This is an integral part of the healing of my wounded soul that I have come here to perform in this lifetime. I am stepping out of the 'box' so to speak and entering the 'paper bag', from strict adherence to all the rules, to bending some and not living in fear of any repercussion from authority. It is time to love me and to dispel all the stories created from my chaotic childhood. I am here to confront, learn and conquer.

It has been made clear to me by a mentor and friend of mine that I no longer need to look for appreciation for what I do. I have taken much time while writing this book to work on the one thing we discovered that was holding back complete love of self. By being the 'good child', I took that role into adulthood where I put myself into situations where I was never receiving the appreciation I was looking for, as I didn't know that was an issue. In less than one minute, this friend pinpointed the situation and reminded me how to revisit the issue, cry the tears, and leave the 'good child' and 'people pleaser' behind where they belong.

My goal here is to guide and to teach others of spirituality as I have learned it, to teach about the power of love and how it helps to heal your suffering heart, if you have not done so already. Everyone who reads this book or listens when I speak at public and private events becomes open to the possibility of learning about the positive effects of self-love. As we know, learning comes in many forms, such as reading, watching videos, surfing the net or listening to an instructor in a classroom setting.

I believe that each unique soul reincarnates repeatedly in order to become divine perfection. Today, I accept this challenge without criticism of myself. Those long-gone days of not loving me have been put to rest, never to resurface in this lifetime or lifetimes to come. This fearless state of self-love, inner peace and tranquility can become a reality for all of us. Once we learn to love ourselves, we will be able to teach others to love themselves and bring peace to the world one day.

As a seeker of self-love, where do you fit into this equation? By reading this book and participating in the exercise of learning to love yourself, you are taking steps to achieve the ultimate triumph on your journey, as I have done; by loving the 'you' in you. Loving you will support what I am trying to accomplish along with the aid of my friends who are invisible to me, my Guides, Angels and Others.

The sacred act of restoration of my mental health was performed with an intensive series of spiritual readings, mediumship, channeling, hypnotherapy, spiritual advising and teaching classes. The most important topic to address being; "Love of Self." I recommend you find a Spiritual Advisor that you trust and work with them. It is not an easy task, but a much needed one if we are to find love of self for all living on Mother Earth. You will glean much information from the books that you read, but discussion and questions are the real answer to your search for enlightenment and self-love. A supportive advisor, mentor, counselor, any name they have given themselves including teacher. Someone you look up to and wish to know their journey with its twists and turns. Realize it could be me that you are most comfortable with.

I ask you also to use the technique of looking into the mirror; look into your soul and lift it out of darkness and sadness and into the light of loving you. I am not pretending that this is an easy task. This is extremely difficult and painful for most of us. It can take many months or, like me, almost three years of revisiting personal pain and working through to forgiveness of me and of the others involved. Looking at yourself and being able to honestly say, "I love you" takes time, courage and conviction. This is not just an easy band-aid, it is an investment in your future. Not only going forward in this lifetime but healing past lifetimes and moving forward into a new incarnation without all of that baggage. Know that as I offer this source to you, it has been one of my major tools on this journey of loving me.

I am conscious of having done restorative work in other lifetimes. Over the years, I have participated in several past life regressions and it all seems to point to a common denominator; I am a healer. I needed to be in love with me to continue my therapeutic journey. I saw myself as a Native American Indian Cave Dweller with my leather pouch of herbs tending to the ill and assisting in the birthing of another soul into our tribe. I was, in one life, crouched behind my vending cart giving a card reading to another woman. By doing this type of work, recuperation takes place as the direction of one's life is shown and crisis in a life of another can be diverted with a different decision.

Everything in my soul's history points to my being a natural healer who has practiced this modality within my many incarnations. During one of our conversations from her new place in the Universe, my mother confirmed that this was in fact true. She has reincarnated with me many times, and her input has been invaluable. This verification was only possible now that my mother and I have been able to establish a rich relationship of love and respect as she resides on the Other Side.

Acknowledge that you are doing exactly what you need to do when sending this soothing energy exactly where it is meant to go.

By recognizing my gifts, I continue my path of loving me. I love myself for my soul's growth and I leave behind the 'people pleaser' embracing where it worked in my life and that it no longer does. I use my healing modalities and subconscious memories to heal me.

There is more to teach you about spirituality and it seems to fit in this chapter as you grow in Spirit and nurture your soul. (Other spiritual information can be found in my initial publication, *It is I, Amadeus, Channeled Messages from Spirit.*)

You may or may not have heard of telepathic communication with another person. Let me explain it. Telepathic communication is what happens when you focus your thinking on another person and set your intention to send them a message straight from your mind, without the assistance of actual words expressed in phone calls, text messages, mail or email.

You concentrate on the message you mean to send without distraction, and its energy is received by the intended recipient.

It is not necessary that the person receiving the message know where it came from, or even acknowledge it. To be able to communicate this message with the person's Higher Self or Team, it is proper to first request permission from their Higher Self so that you are not invading another's space without their consent on some level. In this way, the seed has been planted to be revisited and nurtured to fruition in the future. It might be that you just send them your love, and the receiver smiles quietly as they acknowledge a gentle loving feeling inside themselves.

Other forms of therapy may come in the shape of music or song. The sound of a melody reverberates the restorative energy and then resonates with the individual who needs their heart mended. This can be done with crystal bowls or drumming or your favorite musician. It doesn't matter what instrument is used if the one to be healed is able to feel the vibration. My relationship in this lifetime, with Amadeus Mozart, has become a journey of healing the past and healing the present, using music as therapy for the soul.

When working with someone who has asked to be healed here on Earth, I use one or more modalities. At times, there are many of us simultaneously performing the rectifying work; my Guides, Angels, Elementals and Others, along with those of the person I am working to heal. As always, there is strength in numbers. For example, it has become a pattern on social media that when someone has an illness, and they request a treatment, everyone who reads the post gathers together mentally to send love and light to them in their own time, space and pace, it is a collective curing.

Each month over a previous four-year period, a group of us would gather together at 6:15 p.m. on the last Saturday of the month and send our energy into a container of water. This healing water was then carried by one of us to the ocean where it was gently poured into the waves and sent lovingly adrift to join the healing energy of others. Our common intention with this specific process was to heal the damage caused by the reactors in Fukushima, Japan. Now, we have continued these sessions once a month during my class on Thursday mornings. There are usually five or six of us, but the number is not as important as we all have a common goal. We need all the energy that can be gathered to send into this glass jar. Please feel free to join in and send your energy across the water whenever you can.

As we have been advised by my Guide, Thor, we include all the ills of the world when we send this curative energy and release it into the ocean. It is inevitably received by any person, place or thing that needs to be healed at that moment in time. Thor has advised us that our work has helped, so we continue to perform those collective ceremonies.

We can't control energy, as much as many would like to think we can. We can encase it in wiring and send it across cities, mountains and plains, but should one of the wires snap, that released energy whips everything into a frenzy and has even been known to ignite fires.

Restoration of the soul can also take place during a loving conversation where listening intently and inserting just the right words can heal another's spirit, lifting them from their sadness and despair. I do this often, and with love in my heart, for the soul to which I am tending. Much healing can be accomplished by listening without judgment and helping others to come to healthy conclusions.

It takes tremendous courage to write these words and live the life I have chosen, as it is not for all of us who dwell on this planet. Whatever your beliefs, whenever you openly state them, you expose yourself to being critiqued. My choice to become spiritual came boldly into my life at exactly the right time. I question it at times, as it is still quite new to me; yet it always comes back to my being centered in my decision. Fourteen years is not a long time to be on this path, but whenever I question my beliefs, I hear in my head, "We are with you, now and forever." With these words, love surrounds me, and I know I am home. However, I am not always in step with that which I have previously described. As a soul, living in a human body, having a mortal life, at times I, like all of you, slip back into my humanness and am forced to remind myself to get back on track and work towards being the best I can be by loving the 'me' in me.

Each of us chooses our own path. We have not evolved to the point of not judging others and, occasionally, will criticize that which we don't understand. Over time, I have learned not to judge, yet I have been known to forget that lesson from time to time. I am able to use discernment to keep myself safe and with loving energy of others. Here and now, I stand in the presence of Source Energy, God, Buddha, whatever you may call that which you believe in. With that knowledge, I will stand true to myself and my surroundings on the other side of the veil once my days on Earth are done as they bring comfort to my soul.

Please know I will never try to change your stance on any subject. I am simply here to teach what I have learned and to invite you to dabble in this knowledge to discover if you have experienced something similar to what I have felt. I always implore you to study, research and take into your heart that which resonates with you. Always question. Nobody was born to follow; we were born to make choices that resonate with our own hearts. Yes, I believe we created a life plan for our lives before we arrived at this incarnation, yet we were also given free will. That will can be used to follow the plan according to directives, but also to allow the small stuff to be just that. Changing and rearranging the life plan in small, yet significant ways.

When questions arose, as I began this part of my journey, I sought answers. The resolutions may have come from a class, a teacher, a conversation, a book or from my own personal guides. My Guides, Angels and Elementals; my Team, bring me much joy and confidence in this world. They love me unconditionally. There is no need for them to forgive, they view me as perfection. It's me who has taken all this time to reach a place where I am able to think of myself that way, but self-love is the vital lesson they have taught me and that is how they wish me to feel; exalted by the 'me' that is me and loving me as they do!

It is I, Amadeus. Good morning, Sweet One.

Yes, you are loved. It is so easy for us to love you and stand with you. Your spiritual growth has exceeded all the expectations you ever had regarding your life path. You always questioned the church and eventually quit attending services. It was being taught fear of God and your distaste for the rituals that assisted in this decision. It has been right for you and you will allow others their own paths.

We heard you as a child and a young woman question why you were here, and we heard you speak words that were profound with understanding and knowledge that many needed to glean from books and lectures. You continued this path until you finally discovered our existence. Now, you trust. Now, you feel as though you have found peace in this lifetime.

Love, Amadeus

CHAPTER IV

Loving the 'Me' in Me

I n the previous chapter, I mentioned I used to be a people-pleaser. For most of this lifetime, I have enjoyed this moniker. I used to see myself as someone who was honest, loving and giving, which I honor. However, it bore a huge cost to me. I became lost. Frances became everyone else's fixer and I forgot to take care of me. I am quite sensitive to other people's needs, so it has been easy for me to always play the role of people-pleaser until now.

I must admit, I wasn't always this honest. At about age eight, I broke into the family piggy bank. The goal was to buy candy for my girlfriend and myself, never thinking of the consequences of my actions. Basically, I wanted her to like me, to stay my friend. Just for a change, I wanted to be the one who was able to surprise her with a treat. I didn't see how else to get my hands on any money at that young age. When one does not know to love themselves, buying friends can begin at any age. Maybe some of you see a little of yourselves doing the same thing. It's not uncommon.

The small, rectangular, metal bank sat on top of the bookcase that encased the encyclopedias my parents had purchased from a door to door salesman. The painstakingly saved nickels and dimes were meant to help my parents meet the monthly payments for this educational gift to their children. Neither one ever imagined any of their sons nor daughters would steal that money. And yet, with much strength and ingenuity, and desperation to maintain a friendship, I cracked it open and scooped up its contents.

Once the theft was uncovered, there was an enormous cloud of grief hovering over my house as I arrived home. Honestly, I didn't want to confess to my crimes. Finally, I gave myself up after all of us children were threatened with merciless beatings until the thief turned him/her self in. On the top bunk, I sobbed after the harsh punishment of Dad's cruel belt. This form of childhood torture was meant to teach me a lesson. My subconscious mind filed this episode away. I believed that I was a bad child. The cruel and painful punishment seemed to fit the crime. It proved to me once again that I was not loveable, especially after I had created havoc within my family unit. From being the good child, I suddenly became the bad one, the one who was no longer the pride of my parents' teachings. It also taught me that I was not to expect money to be abundant in my life. Things go along with great stride and money flows and then the current is cut off and things are difficult again. My father felt it his inherent duty to teach me how to live and thrive in society, despite the cost to my inner child. Crushed with humiliation and physical pain, I laid on the bunk crying until I fell asleep.

There are other things I am not proud of; those minor infractions I committed as a young girl and subsequent woman. We all have shameful memories in our lives. However, this is not meant to be a 'tell all' book about my life, but rather to bring an integral part of me into the equation. After all, I am one of the lucky ones who has finally learned how to love herself, and I would like to show you how I did it, and to help you understand how it works. My intention is to show you how far down this long winding road of life I had to come to finally find myself in a position where I could truly love the 'me' in me. If you can understand how my love of self was shattered way back in the beginning of my life, you will be able to more fully comprehend the kind of effort it took to pull it all back together.

This brings me to the time I learned about forgiveness from my teachers and my Team, for this deed and others as they rear their little heads one at a time. I have forgiven myself, and others have exonerated me. I view a certain memory as I recall it, express my forgiveness for the incident, and wrap it in white light, sitting with it for as long as it takes to gradually fade from my consciousness.

Writing one morning and reviewing the above incident, my dad entered my energy field and I wrote, "This is your father and I am aware of what you are working on surrounding the energy of having plenty of money for you and others. The punishment that day was severe and uncalled for. I wish for you to pardon my actions and move forward in abundance." Not an easy thing to do, but it had to be done to propel me forward in my quest for love of me. I forgave him for him and for me.

This method works wonders on the path of loving me. At times, it takes more than one attempt to rid my mind of a long past misdeed, but I visit it as often as it takes for me to acknowledge and recognize my human frailties as just that and walk towards the light of loving me.

I'm extremely fortunate to have my own knight in shining armor; an honorable and forthright man who has taught me, more than anyone else could, about being honest and truthful. My husband, Kevin, has worked diligently throughout the years to guide me on my path, where I could learn to love and believe in myself. He recognizes the broken parts of me, and gently shows me how to put the pieces back together. He assures me that any criticism of a tough piece of asparagus is not my fault as a cook; it's just a tough spear of asparagus. Kevin is my greatest guest at the dinner table where each meal we share receives a resounding, "Thank you, that was delicious". He is my taste-tester in the kitchen and I can count on him to steer me towards the right mix of flavors as he adds his valuable input to the dish.

He, too, had some hard childhood lessons to learn, and he learned them deftly as my friends on the Other Side have told me. (Here, I would like to take a moment to remind you that I am not writing this book alone. 'Deftly' is not a word I am particularly comfortable with, yet, as I refer to my thesaurus, I know this word fits. It is a little used word, but those who guide me have slipped it into this writing, and my love of them caresses it.)

My first marriage failed due to infidelity. I was devastated and felt incredibly insecure. Trying to be open about my feelings, I frequently brought my insecurities into conversations with Kevin. To be honest, until I met him, I truly didn't think I would ever marry again. Yes, of course I dated, but I was going out with all the wrong men. I dated men who were not remotely marriage material at that time in their lives, and consistently felt reassured that I was completely unlovable. In my conscious mind, I conjured up thoughts of unworthiness, spending time with the kind of men who were happy to share their energy with me for a moment, but certainly not a lifetime. They silently declared what I already knew; I was never going to experience the loving security I sought of a lifetime partner, or the assurance that I was filled with self-love.

The first time I married was at the tender age of eighteen. It took several years for me to realize that it had only been my escape route. After high school, my mother prohibited me from moving in with a girlfriend because she perceived me as nothing but a tramp looking for sex. She considered that I would be in a position like hers, at the time when she bore my oldest sister. She'd also been very young. I always cringed at her accusations, as I knew they were not true. As a teenager, I had promised God that I would only ever have one man and one only, so I felt a profound sense of shame when she shouted her vulgar words in apparent disgust.

Back then, I was too young to know that marriage and a baby or two would not be enough for my young husband, who had just come back from Vietnam. The promise I had made to God was broken with the divorce. It hammered my mother's words home. Obviously, I was unlovable, I could see no other reason for the dissolution of my first marriage. One outstanding illustration of the trust I have for Kevin emerged after our second date. It wasn't a date that I would call memorable. We passed the time enjoyably, but rather uneventfully, and, yet, I will remember it always. That night, we dined and danced without fanfare. Barely a word was spoken between us the whole time and, at the end of the evening, feeling slightly perplexed I asked to be taken home.

The following morning, there was a knock on the door. It was Kevin. He asked for a few minutes of my time. I invited him in for coffee, but he refused. He said he had something to tell me. In that instant, my heart dropped. *"Oh, just another one without commitment,"* I thought. Bravely, Kevin explained how he had been seeing someone else for a couple of months, and how much he had been enjoying his time with me. He said he had just come over to tell me that he had broken off the relationship with the other woman that same morning.

"It is 10:30 a.m., you live 40 minutes away from me and you have already accomplished your mission of honestly ending a relationship before actively pursuing another one? Seriously?" I thought. That explained why he was so deep in thought and could not converse the night before. Right before my unknowing eyes, a life changing decision was being made.

Kevin was thirty-two then, and was looking for that special woman, Miss Right, to settle down with and to raise his family. He knew I already had children and hoped to meet them one day. He was willing to take the risk and learn to enjoy them as he enjoyed his time with me. After dating for almost two years, we were married. That was forty years ago. We were still relatively young when we became a family together, and we remain successful in that marriage, raising my two children along with the two we created together. With his heart of gold, Kevin adopted my two children with the permission of their natural father.

I am not saying there have not been obstacles during the forty-two years we have been together, but we have felt it imperative to move through each difficult time with grace and grow old as a couple. A good solid marriage is filled with compromise as two souls unite and find a way to live together in harmony. We are completing a contract that probably began lifetimes ago.

I now realize there were lessons to be learned about my first husband and his family. One of them was his lack of honor towards me, and the fact that I allowed him to get away with his nefarious behavior. To acknowledge that I was meant to be cherished by my husband, not lied to when it was convenient for him, began the journey of loving me although I was not aware of it at the time. It has taken a lifetime for me to arrive at that place, yet that feeling of not being loved unexpectedly rose to the surface once again as he stepped out the front door and out of my life. I cherished the relationship with my ex-husband's family. When we returned to Tucson, which was often since my family lived there, Kevin would suggest we visit my ex-husbands family so they could see the children. At those times, we would sip a drink of something and share cheese and crackers. So, it was, through my marriage to him, I was enjoying a relationship with others in my soul group.

There are many more instances over the past four decades where Kevin proved his devotion such as making sure that my children were included in our life together by playing with them, hugging and kissing them and expressing his love for them. He sat in the kitchen as I prepared the evening meal and asked me about my day listening attentively as often as he could. He traveled to other states during his employment and called each night to say he loved me and wished me pleasant dreams. With Kevin in my life, I gradually began to trust again, particularly after the experience of my devastating divorce and the bad boys I had dated in the eighteen months following it until meeting my life partner. Kevin taught me to honor the loving connection we had created together, and I became more and more trusting and trustworthy, modeled in his image. Our loss of Damon hit my husband as hard as it hit me. He grieves alongside of me to this day.

As we examine briefly why I identified with being a loving people-pleaser, we get closer into my heart as it grows in a feeling of oneness with my Higher Self and Source. As a young wife and mother, I firmly believed that I could raise a family surrounded with love, and that I could teach my children they are truly loved. I trusted that I could shift the paradigm. I was sure that my children would be enabled to move through their lives on a path of love, in turn loving their own children unconditionally.

So far, I have witnessed that ability in all of them. My daughter, Michelle, has one son and has mothered a step-son and step-daughter. The blending of families is not always easy, but she has done a fabulous job of it alongside her husband. Their two boys live in Tucson, and their daughter lives in California. Michelle has had a lot of fun with all her children, even though her step-children lived with their mother most of the time. Every time they could visit, it was a treat to have them over and operate as a loving family unit.

Next came Damon. His daughter, Morgan, was eight years old when he left the Earth. As explained much earlier in another chapter, Damon died of a heart attack, completely unexpected, at the age of 33. He was present at his daughter's birth and for the first year of her life. Before her first birthday, however, his wife had moved on to a new man, and a comparatively civil divorce followed. The change in circumstances did not prevent Damon from spending as much time as he could with the love of his life. On weekends and during vacations, he picked up his little girl and took her to his house or ours. There, he would play with her on the floor and she would sit on his back. Other times they would spend endless hours retrieving colored toothpicks from the bottom of the pool. Anything for his Angel. She couldn't get enough of him. Ultimately, as he drifted into death in the middle of the night, this close physical relationship with his daughter ended. But their connectedness is alive and well. He parents and watches over her from the Other Side. Because of her mother being a single parent, without backup, and needing time for herself, Kevin and I had Morgan with us many weekends. We have formed a strong bond that can never be broken.

My third child, Kevin II, has two little ones with another on the way. I know he and his wife will never look back on their ability to love their children unconditionally. They are both confident and filled with love and light for the future of their little family. Their amazing boys have been surrounded with love from every direction from the moment they were born and, as they grow, they are being nurtured with all the blessings of being with Mom and Dad, and their unconditional love. Their new sibling will have the same love. She will join her brothers and they will laugh and play and bond.

Lastly, my youngest son, Sean, and his wife have a son and have moved quickly and easily into the role of responsible loving parents. They are extremely comfortable in their skins as Mom and Dad and love comes easily to this laughing little guy. We look forward to watching them parent and grow together.

As I stumbled through my own journey, I did all I could do; hug, kiss, hold and express verbally my love for these four beautiful souls, my children. When they were young, I played with them whenever I could, and nurtured them all, to the best of my ability, during their developing years. When my oldest began kindergarten, being the consistent knowledge seeker that I am, and aware of the kind of mother I wanted to become, I sought out parenting classes at the elementary school. These classes helped to reinforce my ability to love my children well, sustain their fragile inner child, while simultaneously building up strength of character in each of them so they could withstand whatever bumps and bruises life might have in store for them. They needed to function in society, yet make love of self an important part of their souls.

By taking classes, I learned how to support my children's decisions and to encourage them to become respectful humans who could support themselves in their lives here on Earth. Now, I can proudly say that my original goal has been more than accomplished. Did I make mistakes? Of course I did! Just ask any one of my them! As with all things we must learn, there are many disappointing moments when you wish you knew then what you know now.

Despite my inexperience with unconditional love, I did my best to teach each one of my children, boldly and openly, that they were truly loved. I taught them to do their best, know that they had given it all they had. After each little success, they could look back on the path they had traveled and be deservedly pleased with their progress. This strange concept of learning to love the 'me' in me is still quite new to their Mom so, unfortunately, it was not actually taught to them. That being said, I feel they do love themselves.

When I broached the subject of them loving themselves now, my two boys rolled their eyes, told me I did a great job of raising them, and turned up the music. Damon, who is in Spirit, enjoys knowing that I am bringing this topic up with them, as well as sharing my knowledge with his daughter. Michelle is on her spiritual journey. Unlike her brothers, she fully comprehends the concept of loving herself completely. She and I have taken the time to have profound conversations about her innermost thoughts. We enjoy a solid and loving relationship that has matured in time as she is no longer a child. Knowing I did the best I could with what I knew makes me comfortable. After all, that is exactly what my parents did, right or wrong. I'm lucky to have been blessed with so many wonderful opportunities to learn from the uncertainty of childhood, and now to have learned to leave it all behind.

I have found that discussing the giving parts of myself is rather difficult. As I give others my shoulder to cry on, my ear to listen to their woes and my love to help them heal, I, too, cry both openly and on the inside. At times, the appalling stories I have heard from people who have sought my help have made me shudder. There is such untold sadness in the world. As an Empath, I can physically feel the pain of others.

For many years, I have healed others of their distress only to feel their pain ripping into my soul. Now, after much suffering, I have learned how to shield myself from people's anguish so that I am able to better help them relieve their sorrows without allowing their agonies into my energy field. After each healing session, I take a minute to close my eyes and move my own soul into a new and loving space especially reserved for me. Even though, at the beginning of each session, I set the intention to be safe from the ailments of my clients and to not take on any aspect of any negative energy they may have. It's necessary to do this for my own peace of mind.

Now it is time to teach my grandchildren the same wonderful thing that I have so recently learned; to love themselves. Their parents love them yet by teaching them to be safe in the world, negative verbiage can be used. It is as simple as 'no', 'don't, 'stop it'. Depending on the strength of the voice, the child begins to doubt love even without knowing it.

It is Justine, Dear Sweet One.

I have stepped forward this day to help you lessen any feelings of sadness or pain you may have suffered from the energy that 'ripped through your soul' as you have so lovingly written.

You have learned to be grounded, protected and at peace while you counsel, listen and heal others. It has been our pleasure to help you through this place of pain and sorrow and to direct you to the sources that have taught you all that you needed to know. We are pleased that you have heard and heeded our words. We work quietly here, without judgment. We are extremely gratified when you hear us, and pay attention to the niggling (ha, ha, not my word!) sensation that reminds you to pull every-thing together.

You chose to learn from the chaos. Now, you have learned so much you are able to counsel others. *To experience those negatives has enabled you to expect the best and recognize it when it appears right in front of you. The best came to you as the soul energy that is Kevin, and he has been set to cross your path, so he can help you to see the truth of what love is. Not only the physical, but also the fathomless care and honor that you have experienced. Love him and be grateful each day for his presence.*

The older grandchildren love you and look to you for pure love without judgment. You can do this now. The young ones and those to come will be excited to be in your loving energy as you teach them love of self.

Go in love, light, laughter and peace, Justine

CHAPTER V

Try to Give up Passing Judgment

N ow you know something about me; who I once was, and who I am becoming now. The journey these days is easy and loving. Remembering not to harshly judge myself is trying, at times, as I move forward to make it a habit. There are still moments when I forget to love me and slip back to a place where I am trying to please others. As soon as I recognize this people-pleasing energy, I quickly rearrange my thoughts and move forward. It is not that I won't ever try to please someone with a special birthday gift or a surprise, but it is no longer about them loving me just because of my gift or loving deed. It is simply because they enjoy what is being presented. There's a big difference, and I am grateful to the Universe to have learned what that is.

At times, I can't help but smile when I perform a kind deed for another person, and quickly remind myself that I did it for them. Not so that I would be looked upon as "that gracious woman in the checkout line who gave up her space". That is now nothing more than a passing notion and I move swiftly forward without any judgment, good or bad. Also, I do not expect anyone to say, "thank you." If gratitude is offered, it is accepted, but I feel I must be able to give freely without any motivation whatsoever based on the energy of those words. Now, that is hard! I have been drilled by my parents to offer and expect thanks. It feels slightly weird to abandon those expectations. However, knowing that by giving from the heart, the gift is simply a gift. It needs no recognition to still be the present which is, in itself, an offering.

It has been extremely difficult to break another one of those bad habits we all tend to have. By loving myself, I can no longer say to myself, "You are so dumb. Why did you do that?" I must catch those thoughts before they get loose, and try to remember that, by uttering a derogatory statement like that, I am passing judgment on *my* very essence.

Many of us are guilty of this. I hear it every day. And I wish it to end for all of us. After over-hearing someone I know admonish themselves, I will often say; "I don't have any stupid friends, so I really don't know who you are talking about." That statement pulls us back into a moment of love, without a long discussion, and usually brings about some playful laughter. Just yesterday, a dear friend called herself stupid. I questioned her about it and she told me she says that all the time! I reminded her to love herself and will gift her with a copy of this book as soon as it is published. We all need to stop having negative thoughts about ourselves. These thoughts serve no purpose. All they do is reinforce the negative and make us feel unworthy of real love.

It feels magical to step into oneness and say I am perfect. At the same time, it also feels so foreign. I was born perfect and bask in the remembrance of being born that way, without being out of alignment with Ego. I am worthy of the love I have discovered in this lifetime. It is not something I am remembering from a life before this one. It is now. Therefore, I have followed my own story as I stepped into my family, my first marriage, my second marriage, the passing of my son, the growth of my children and grandchildren. Everything. The story had to be this way to finally arrive at the moment when I get to bask in self-love. To get to today.

I imagine you are wondering what this type of love and perfection feels like. That's the reason I am asking you to allow me to guide you through the process. With your permission, I will gently escort you on this segment of your journey. The process can be slow and wrought with feelings of discontent, and it is not without setbacks. Yet, each step we take during our lifetime leads us to the place where we are meant to be. It may seem like a daunting task to undertake, but the outcome is divine.

Up until this moment, you may have revisited many painful episodes in your life. As you recall these unpleasant times, know that the main thing is to be looking at them, not with judgment, but instead with forgiveness. These memories can no longer hurt you. By forgiving past transgressions, you release your soul from its chains of pain and anger. In turn, this softens the blows caused by the infliction of that old unhealthy energy.

Absolution has nothing to do with the person you are pardoning, including yourself. The act of forgiveness is meant to relieve you of the pain you feel when you conjure up those terrible memories that brought you into a place of not loving you. Forgiving helps to bring you into a place of light, where those recollections no longer resurface with that old blaze of raw, agonizing energy. If they enter your mind at all, you will be able to move quickly from old thought patterns, directly into love of you.

I'd like to take this time to explain how the soul feels pain and anger. In each lifetime, the soul experiences different emotions; conflicts or pure love. It takes what it needs from the lessons presented at that time, using this knowledge to grow and expand. This energy remains in the subconscious so that one does not have to relearn the lesson in a future lifetime. For example: My mother, while on the Other Side, was still having great difficulty forgiving herself for an action in her most recent lifetime. Over several sessions, she and I worked together to bring her to the point of self-acceptance and forgiveness. She had to admit to her atrocity and seek forgiveness from me. Without this additional healing work, she would have been forced to return to the lesson once again in a future incarnation. By doing this, and working through the difficulties, we have settled this issue once and for all. So, I want you to understand that we still work on our shortcomings even while on the other side immersed in the energy of Source.

Now, I would like you to wrap your mind around the concept that you won't ever have to revisit any of the pain that this life may have inflicted upon you. Earlier in this missive, I explained how to visit a painful action and wrap white light around it until it was gone. After you have done that, you can allow yourself a blanket of forgiveness for any unkind acts that you feel may have hurt others, and also for anything hurtful they may have done to you, as tiny as they may be. You can begin this practice by wrapping yourself in a bubble of white light and sitting quietly until the light becomes a pink fluffy cloud that settles around you, cloaking you in a rich love vibration, and a deep inner peace which you may have never felt before.

This great feeling of deep satisfaction within your soul does not mean that you will not trip or falter at times. I still stumble occasionally. I am not righteously claiming that I never overreact, or show impatience, or gossip, or inadvertently slip. In the past, this would have been a good reason to mentally beat myself up. Floundering from time to time simply means I understand the feeling of living in a state of 'self-loathing' and can gently return myself to the place of self-love upon realizing my error because I have known this love vibration in this lifetime.

Even if you have just learned of the possibility of this peaceful calm only five minutes ago, it will not ever completely leave you again. I have found, with practice, that I am now able to return to love of self in a heartbeat, and so can you once you've achieved it! Once you have experienced this love, you will relish this feeling. The best time is right now. Don't wait another moment ... dive in and practice until you feel a sense of joy and bliss like you have never known before. It's also important to realize that you may find you cannot do this work alone. There are many of us doing this same kind of work all over the world. You've come this far. It's time to do the steps to come to love of self.

Understanding and recognizing any negative thoughts you may have of yourself is one of the first steps in self-healing. Truly comprehending that you wrote your own journey and its accompanying lessons, before you came into the body, you now encompass–is of vast importance. At one point, you sat with a counsel on the Other Side, and you agreed to return once more to the Earth and continue your journey of growth and enlightenment. Those souls who agreed with this incarnation and what was to be accomplished are the same ones you chose for your parents, siblings and friends. They also include co-workers, teachers and all your ex's. (This also refers to ex-friends, ex-bosses, etc.) Whether you remain close to any of them is not relevant. Simply that you met up with them as part of your life experience is what I am referring to.

That you have had an experience with them in this lifetime may help to clear up differences in past incarnations.

Perhaps you have been advised at some point that you can change the direction of your life. Yes, it is true that you have been gifted with free will. But, when you are committed to a lesson with full conviction, you will see that all the people who have been present in your life during this incarnation have helped in some way to bring you to the place where you are today.

The overprotective, abusive or critical parent, the obstinate teacher, the sarcastic boss, the unruly sibling, the cheating spouse or significant other have all been purposefully set onto your path to determine whether you are going to learn the lesson this time around, or if you are going to keep bumping your head against the same painful wall.

The plan also includes that grade school teacher who understood you and helped you find your way, your best friend forever, your loving partner, parent or relative, the mentor who helped you out of the heap and into the center stage of your life. Whether we remember them or not, we all have at least one someone in our lives who has touched us with love, enough for us to know that we also want it for ourselves.

Are you ready to move forward and love yourself? Are you ready to properly deal with these misguided souls who hurt you, without casting your own judgment upon the situation or their energy? Are you ready to thank those who gave you a lift when you were down? Are you ready to embark on a new path, take a new direction? And learn to love the 'you' in you? Are you ready to make life changing leaps and bounds? If so, this book has been placed in your hands by Spirit with your permission.

The effort you put into repairing your soul will come back to you with resounding rewards. It may also come with the ending of relationships that do not serve you well. Remember, these relationships have been elected for closer scrutiny by you and your magnificent team on the Other Side, to assist you along the path of spiritual growth. If it comes to this point, someone you have chosen to leave behind may not understand the end of this connection with you. It may cause them a great deal of pain.

When that time comes, it is not for you to judge, just discern. The person you are cutting ties with came to assist you in some way, and this portion of their journey may be ended, albeit gracefully.

I am not suggesting you make a rude departure, unless that is what is being asked of you by your Higher Self. Leaving gently is best; fewer phone calls and visits, which you may have found caustic to your own love of self, will send a gentle message to the soul you are choosing to relinquish that their work with you is done.

This is your story. You get to fill each blank page as it unfolds, and it is not for someone else to step in and tell you exactly how to write it. It is yours alone to learn. With that in mind, don't accept any information being presented to you by another soul if you have not specifically asked for it. Anyone claiming to be psychic or not, can enter another person's energy field without permission, unless you have protected that space. I implore you to use the protection that will be revealed to you in a following chapter. Permission is vital to you being able to perceive what resonates and what does not.

If you pass a message onto anyone without their permission, it may cause an angry backlash. Asking to move forward can be as simple as, "May I share something with you?" At times, it can be difficult to stop yourself from blurting out information that you are picking up while in someone else's energy field, especially when you are just learning about your new gifts. In time, you will learn to control the incoming messages and have conversations that do not impose your gifts on others. You don't have to listen to what is coming to you from the Other Side. If you feel confused or overwhelmed, you can give yourself permission to ask your Team to step away and take a break for a while. As you become accustomed to the practice, you will find it is more fun to have engagements with others and enjoy the surprise of the outcome.

I am Justine, Lovely Lady.

I have come to shower you with love. We are so pleased with the way you are learning this lesson of love of self. It has never been brought to you in previous lifetimes. It is only now that

Amadeus and the rest have come to bring this to you.

You have evolved in the many times you have reincarnated, and we wish for this to be a time of devout love for you. As you learn and teach others, a powerful vibration circles the Earth and you will know that you have touched the lives of many. Teaching all who read this book, or those you chatter with, will benefit from the sage advice of asking for consent before passing on a message. This is crucial information for them.

You are to be commended for remembering to point that out to those who are just beginning to use their powerful skills, and that they must proceed in utmost respect of all others. As you are teaching them, you are also reminding yourself to do the same. You are human and do forget occasionally, so this is a good time to bring this topic to the forefront for all who are listening, including yourself. Do not falter in this new sensation. Keep it close to your heart and your mind. Remind yourself often that all that exists proves itself to be loving to heal the Earth. Enjoy the vibration of this day.

Love, Justine.

CHAPTER VI

Learning to Meditate and Write Automatically

"What is automatic writing and why do I want to learn about it?" you may well ask. Let's begin by following the path I took on my journey. It was an interesting time in my life where I was exposed to souls who belonged to the spiritual community at every turn. The women I worked with were sharing what they knew. A friend of many years talked about Yogananda's teachings, and about following his word. A woman who purchased a home and hired me as her interior designer told me she was psychic. They seemed to be surfacing for a reason unknown to me at the time. On October 26, 2003, to be exact, I was hit by a devastating event. I will not go into the finer details but, on that day, my son left this world far too soon for my heart. Yes, gone too soon. Age: thirty-three. Cause: heart attack.

As this brutal reality set in, I found myself going to work and coming home. My work consumed me, yet I continued learning spiritually from those at work, and enjoying the calmness that surrounded me. A friend at work had a sister who is a psychic/intuitive, so I met with the woman and enjoyed her company.

This psychic read for many of my friends. As we got to know each other, she decided to teach a meditation class in Costa Mesa. My friend, Lynn, accompanied me for support as I dove tentatively, for the first time, into the pool of meditation and beyond.

We sat quietly in our chairs as a stray cat wove his way between our legs, before finally settling on my feet. We were instructed to close our eyes, uncross our legs and arms and lay our palms up in our laps. Some people took off their shoes, but there was a cat warming my feet, and I didn't want to disturb either of us.

The teacher began a guided meditation. We had previously been told that, while she was guiding us, if our minds took us somewhere else, we should just follow whatever we were seeing or doing. She led us into a meadow and to a stream. She asked us to visualize wildlife, energy and spirit. I saw nothing.

Excitedly, other students talked about what they saw, smelled and heard. One saw fairies and gnomes romping among the leaves of small plants. Some walked with butterflies flitting among fields of colorful flowers. I repeat, I got nothing. Absolutely nothing. "Hmmm, what was that about, I wondered?"

The meditations were the same each week. Soon, I called the teacher to chat and she assured me that of course I had seen things, but I wasn't yet ready to trust that it was real. She carefully assured me that, in time, as I began to trust and not dwell in a place where I felt I wasn't good enough, I would be able to write what I saw. She explained that most of the others had meditated before and had already learned to believe in their visions. Reassured, I agreed to return for another month.

It took some time for me to relax and have faith. It took time to trust in the practice I was being shown. One day, the light bulb inside my mind flashed with reality! Finally, I was able to see! I had learned to quit editing whatever was going on in my mind during a session. When asked to visualize, I trusted there was a meadow, a stream and an energy visiting me during our guided meditations. Alas, in the beginning, the energy was just a shape without substance, but it was definitely there! Week after week, my friend and I attended meditation class. Gradually, I learned to relax in my meditations at home. My friend Lynn had accomplished what she came to do, so she stopped coming to class with me. She could now meditate on her own at home, and that was really all she was looking for. She had been there for me to lean on just as I got started, and I was now strong enough to go it alone.

After a few months of this class, we were asked to bring a journal to the next class. We would begin to explore Automatic Writing. We would learn to trust what we saw and heard during our meditations and write down our observations when it had ended. I bought a spiral notebook at the drug store and, that next Tuesday, was off to class. I was no longer insecure in my abilities. The wonderment I felt in knowing that all my life I had been receiving information and ignoring it as though they were unwanted thoughts of my own volition! I had Guides and Angels and Elementals surrounding me asking me out of pure non-judgmental love to listen and heed their advice. The unspoken words had been with me this lifetime and I was now able to hear them and know that through this Team on the Other Side I was becoming the very best that I could conjure up in this incarnation.

After almost three months, I discovered I had developed and honed my ability to walk through the meadow and sit by the water and see the creatures who came into my guided meditations. There is usually a red fox and a chipmunk with me during these times. I see my Guides and/or Angels as they enter the meditation, and I receive the gifts they have brought with them. I am able to feel their loving presence, and I try to sit in that moment for as long as I can. Before all the pieces came together, I had learned to trust. Not to the depth I would learn later, but enough to welcome the messages that filter through to me during these meditations.

The most fascinating gift I received in those early days was a quill and a small decanter of ink from one of my Guides. When the instructor heard about this gift, she said, "They want you to write." Write what? I wondered. In my journal? "That seems preposterous," I thought. At that time, I was already writing in my journal as often as life would allow. I would try to begin each morning with a mediation and journaling session, but if I missed, there was always midday or evenings. Usually I found time five or six days each week for many months as I was overjoyed with the contact with my Team and the direction my life was taking. My pain and loneliness of losing my son at that time of my life began to become bearable and the tears that had flowed so often had abated somewhat. The teacher then went on to explain that it seemed my path was to write books at their request.

The following morning, as I reread what I had written the night before, I got such a surprise to see words I generally never use scrawled across the pages. I was overjoyed! While writing, I had allowed those on the Other Side to use my mind and hands to bring their messages to life. This was the very beginning of trust.

I want to clarify here, that I do not perform any of the rituals of sitting rigid, feet flat on the floor, or holding my palms upwards. When I sit in my living room or on my patio, I allow my meditation to relax me and invite in Spirit. (In fact, when I teach, I advocate that you only need be present.) If you wish to add your own personal rituals to your meditations, that is your choice. In my personal meditations, it is just me and them. I am at peace, and I have set aside sufficient time to calm myself and tune my mind in, so I can listen to the messages of the day being passed to me by my unseen friends. They may be answering a question, or just giving me a message about something coming into my path in the future. I have learned to trust all that happens and to let it flow.

Over time, I allowed the pen in my hand to be commandeered by these new friends in my life. I no longer have control over the penmanship I was so pleased with during my lifetime as it disappears at times. Now, I have allowed each Guide or Angel to use my mind and my hand to bring their messages to life in my journal. As written previously, each entity comes with their own energy and style of hand writing. Oh, the journals I have filled! After more than a year, I wrote and wrote with them each day, finally deciding there was more to the writing than I had originally thought. There were so many messages, I was not surprised when the idea formed to present them to the world. Clearly, it was time for me to write a book.

For about two years, I wrote and wrote and copied paragraphs directly from my journals into the blank pages on my computer. Everything I had been taught during the last few years by those on the Other Side was typed into my laptop and then sorted into chapter after chapter. It was a long and tedious road.

Finally, editing began. I chose Jean-Noel Bassior to be my editor. I had taken her class a year or more before and I resonated with her energy. Jean-Noel had been a journalist who interviewed celebrities and others during her career. I felt trepidation as I wrote that first email to her. She was quite well known. Why would she consider editing my work? You get it, don't you? At that point, I still didn't feel worthy. I hadn't yet reached a place where I had learned to love me. To my great surprise, Jean-Noel responded in a timely manner. I was elated with her response. She agreed to assist me. While we were chatting, she revealed that she was doing some editing, working with a friend on a television show, and pursuing some new adventures. She accepted the position I offered her, and we took exactly one year to rework my draft.

The time it took to polish this book was an individual choice. Bringing the book to fruition was a long slow process. It was possibly fear of success or maybe fear of failure. I never quite decided exactly what had held me back, but one day it was completed. At the precise moment the Universe intended, I moved forward with publication.

Jean-Noel was patient and incredibly knowledgeable! Here I was, a first-time writer, and she, a seasoned veteran. She teased me about sending her my first draft, and I just smiled to myself. How could she have known the hours I had put in to this, or about the four people who had read it and provided valuable input, promoting many drafts? It was the best version I had at that time.

My editor schooled and challenged me in ways I had never been tested She taught me the questions I should ask after writing a paragraph, and how to answer those questions. If they couldn't be answered, the paragraph had to be rewritten to make sure that I was really allowing the reader to enjoy the flow. She taught me much more as the work progressed, but I am not here to talk about how to become an editor. I am a storyteller.

Thus, my first book, *It is I, Amadeus: Channeled Messages from Spirit,* came tumbling into publication in June of 2014.

Jean-Noel brought out the very best in my work. I wrote to her and offered first right of refusal as the editor of my new book. She has moved on to other huge projects as I write this, so a new editor has stepped in, never knowing how much easier the job will be thanks to the training of this woman I now call a friend. Roni Askey-Doran was sent to me by the Universe as my current editor for the alignment of her story of love of self as I journeyed through mine. She will still have plenty of corrections for me, I'm sure. My perfection is not in writing the story, it is in believing I deserve to share my story, and my love of self.

Part of the agreement I made, before I entered this lifetime, was to write books and share messages with the world. Did I know that until now? Absolutely not. Do I believe it to be true? Resoundingly, yes!

It is I, Amadeus, Dear One.

Good morning, as you greet the day! You, Dear One, are so busy writing that I don't wish for you

to forget to play. Tomorrow will be the most playful day of your month. The Holistic Faire you participate in takes a lot of energy, but you do so enjoy the energy of the others. Your favorite part of the day is when you speak to the audience. Sometimes they fill the room, sometimes they do not. But, you always have control of you and enjoy bringing me to talk and answer their questions.

The messages that come from me are for all of them to hear, and for you as this day there is no time to sit, meditate and journal with the bustle of activity all around. Listen to their applause and know that what you are giving to them is a gift unlike any other they will receive in this lifetime.

You will talk of self-love, but you will also answer their questions about what is affecting them in this lifetime. Each time you give an answer, know that it resonates with everyone in the room.

There is so much for you to teach, one soul at a time. This feels daunting to you, but know that as each one you teach grows, and begins teaching others, your job will take on an easier energy. Also know that we have invited many others to learn to love themselves and to teach this message. You are not alone. As you move through the day, remove all judgment and let the energy flow. We remind you of this from

time to time as you are human and sometimes forget the lessons you have learned.

Go in love, light AND laughter, Amadeus.

CHAPTER VII

Grounding, Protection, Intention & Meeting Amadeus

Now is a good time to remind you that when you are learning about something new, it's vitally important to find a teacher whose energy you enjoy, and who makes you feel safe within the confines of the classroom. The most influential thing a teacher can do is challenge a student and empower him/her to ask more questions and to dig deeper. I wish for each of you to continue your quest for the answers to your questions. There are multiple sources available where you can glean the information that you seek. Ask questions until you are comfortable with the answers. This is your responsibility. Do not take your beliefs lightly. You and you alone are the keeper of your soul. What you choose to believe in is entirely up to you.

The first thing I had to discover when exploring automatic writing was the concept of 'trust'. This is a very deep and conscious feeling of knowing. Know that you are surrounded by Guides, Angels, Elementals and Others. They are with you throughout your lifetime. They carry with them a powerful and everlasting love that will help you learn the lessons you are here on this planet to discover. Some are with you for a selected purpose and usually leave when the job is completed. Some will stay for a lifetime and some of them are with you for many lifetimes. You have been entrusted to their care. Hence, it's vital to learn to trust, trust, trust whatever these energies are teaching you. This Team comes to you with blessings from the Other Side and they act only out of love.

As I promised earlier, I will share how I learned to ground myself and how to protect myself when it is necessary. This is a good lesson to follow. If you begin by grounding yourself to the Earth the first thing each morning, you will find much peace in your day. You can do this exercise anywhere. You might do it as you open your sleep rested eyes before your feet hit the floor or you might find yourself remembering to do this as you sit at the breakfast table after showering and dressing, getting ready to move through another day of joy and gratitude.

First, close your eyes and thank the Universe for its gifts. Now, imagine a heavy cord or thick tree root growing from the base of your spine, at your root chakra, and watch it travel through the Earth to its very core; this core is known as Gaia.

Now, observe as it wraps itself around Gaia. Keep your energy close to you. Sit quietly in this space for a few minutes and feel the energy moving in closer towards your body. You are able to send any negative thoughts you may be carrying through this cord to Gaia, and she will transmute the energy into all things positive and send it back to you.

To protect this energy, try to visualize a sturdy metal plate in front and behind you. Picture it as shiny and beautiful as near to you as feels comfortable. Some choose plexiglass with its transparency making them feel more at ease with this new sensation. Decorate your protective shield with crystals and glitter if you wish! By setting up strong boundaries, your energy cannot be utilized or intruded upon by others with whom you may engage with during your day. Also, know you will not be giving away your energy, but keeping it to yourself, to enhance your own strength, as you interact with other people who, knowingly or unknowingly, try to use your energy to lift themselves up. As your beliefs grow and evolve, you will not need either this exercise or the grounding one quite as often. It will become easier to set the intention of positivity and protection in your mind, after a few moments of sitting in gratitude for all that you have.

There is much innocence in the world. Without knowing anything about energy, whether it is yours or another person's, some may delight in what they feel while they are around you and feel the urge to sit with you, so they can share what feels so good to them. This can be rocky ground, as they may unknowingly intrude on your energy. When moments like that arise, it is up to you to activate your protection. Most people don't even know they are doing it, but it's possible they are making you restless. You may feel the need to scoot away from them. There is nothing harmful in this action if you recognize what is going on. Just put your shields or intentions in place and continue to move through your day. Know that they are not bad people, just uninformed about the way energy is processed.

Set the intention that the practices you are going through are for your highest and best good, and that you are completely safe in this endeavor. Go to a quiet space where you have a notebook and pen lying nearby. Still your mind by concentrating on your breathing. Let go of Ego (a person's sense of self-esteem or self-importance). It is easier to set your persona aside now that you know you can. Begin breathing in and out with a peaceful rhythm of in through the nose and out through the mouth. Understand that you may hear chatter, and random thoughts may interrupt your concentration. Gently continue to move back to the words, "Breathe in, breathe out."

Continue paying close attention to your breathing until there is stillness. It is then that you are most receptive to messages. Without thought or question, write down the words you hear. The key here is Trust with a capital 'T'. Even if the message sounds disjointed or is unlike anything you are used to hearing or saying, know that it is coming from Source and from those who love you unconditionally. They won't do anything to hurt you. They have only your best interests at heart.

It may take weeks or even months of practice to attain a higher level of awareness. Sometimes it is easier with a guided meditation, where someone leads you into the stillness required for the mind to completely accept the quiet, and to hear the words being spoken. From that point, the rest is up to you. You are in control of all that enters your energy field. As you set the intention of only goodness and love speaking to you, that is all you will hear.

You will become more comfortable sitting down to write with these loving energies the more time you spend with them. If you wish, begin the day with a question on your note pad. They will bring you the answer with the same sage advice they have always given you. It is up to you to trust this information is not being invented by your mind but is actually coming from your Team.

Once you have learned how to receive the messages, you will be actively receiving the advice being given. Don't ignore its subtle influence. It's quite common for your Team to remind you not to forget to take something with you, such as a diary or notepad. You may hear their message as a thought, then ignore it and think you will grab the book later. Unknowingly, you leave the house for class and remember somewhere along the way there that you've forgotten your notebook. Then, you will double back to retrieve it arriving late or attend class unprepared. Listen and trust. When they pass along a message like that, immediately follow the instructions. Keep the notebook near your car keys so you always have it and save yourself much angst.

Know that, at any time, you can ask anyone on your Team to slow down their words as you write, or to be more specific with their messages. These loving energies do not take offense to anything you say or request. Remember, unconditional love for you is all they know. Since they do not exist in the Earth's energy of time and space, they simply act with pure love.

As I learned to trust, I saw a wizened old man dressed in white robes with sandals on his feet. This vision took place during a guided meditation with my teacher. He was standing in a gazebo. I heard what I thought to be the name, "Armadeus." I began daily meditations with the breathing I have taught to you and continued to write down messages I had received directly from Armadeus.

After re-reading, everything I had written in the days that followed each of these meditations, I realized with a jolt that these words were not from me at all. This text was filled with words I didn't usually use. Certainly, it was not my handwriting. There were phrases I recognized, but they were not a normal part of my daily vocabulary. This entity seemed to have similar characteristics to mine. I smiled, as he was the first to come through with a message during the classes I attended. In any class, I take an active part in as a student, you will usually find me near the front of the room. I am often the first to raise my hand to read or participate. This was exactly what he was doing, and I knew then, with certainty, that he had been with me for many years.

When he first came through, "Armadeus" always announced his presence with the following words: I*t is I, "Armadeus"*. This is what I thought I heard. It took some time before I was to learn that it was Amadeus. (The other Guides and Angels would, in time, develop their own personal introductions, too.) For many months, I wrote with whom I thought was "Armadeus", until one day, out of curiosity and at the urging of a student who was musically gifted, I asked during meditation for clarity, and so it was given. I asked and heard, Wolfgang Amadeus Mozart. There was my answer, the truth, which may have never been known, or certainly not for a long time, had I not listened to the request of the student and trusted the words that I heard. My belief says that this student had been presented to me precisely to bring Amadeus to the forefront of who he was.

"Yes, I was Wolfgang Amadeus Mozart in one of my past lives, and this is the name I am using for you to connect with me.

You see, where my spirit energy still exists, we have no need for names to communicate with each other. We are energy souls and take no real form. When I come to you, you need to hear a name to identify which energy is coming to you at any given time. So, it is that I have chosen Amadeus, as it is a strong name. And my past lifetime as Wolfgang Amadeus Mozart is chronicled as being extremely gifted with my music and extremely prolific with my voice. It is unto you that I will be unfolding many words of wisdom, as you work with others to heal their pain and their wounds on this earth plane incarnation of the soul, known this lifetime as Frances."

Shocked at this answer, I questioned why someone so famous had come to be with me. There it was ... my lack of love of me was showing up once again. (This took place in 2010 and I had first heard from him in 2007.) Amadeus told me that he had been with me for many lifetimes, and that I had proved to be quite a handful! I laughed, knowing exactly what that meant. I am pleased he remained with me over and over.

It took over seven years to find out exactly why he had stuck with me. It is a truly delightful story that is covered in another chapter. You will smile when you read this part of my story. Trust me. If you have enjoyed this book thus far, you will enjoy discovering the reason Amadeus is my Master Guide.

Once you have conquered automatic writing during this lifetime, should you choose this path, and begin to ask questions of these loving energies, you will gradually realize that the answers you have received will help to direct your life in a positive direction. That is how I developed my first book which was published in June 2014.

It is I, Amadeus, Dear One.

It is so nice to be with you more regularly these days. We are writing a book. All of us are pleased with the progress and your dedication to this project. It is more about them ('them' means you, the reader) *than you, Sweet One.*

We treasure seeing you research and find the answers to your own questions. We love that you know how to research, and that it is important for your truth. Teaching our readers to ground and protect is crucial for all, but most importantly for those who are empathetic. Empaths tend to avoid crowds as they absorb the energy around them more quickly than others. You are truly blessed to be an Empath, and with what you have learned through your journey thus far, you can now move without fear into any space. Claustrophobia is no longer an energy for you to own since you learned to protect yourself and shared that knowledge in this chapter.

We are truth when we write with you. You are loving you on a more regular basis. Go within and feel the bliss. Fly through this day in love, light and laughter.

Love, Amadeus

CHAPTER VIII

And Then I Became a Channel

Did I ever imagine that I wanted to channel? No. I didn't even really know what that meant until the evening our teacher told us that channeling would be the next sector of the class. She then explained how it works and detailed the process in which we could achieve this gift.

Why did I agree to move forward with this class when I could so easily have dropped out? I was so thrilled with my progress in my new world of spirituality that I wanted more. This new direction had taken me away from the work treadmill, where I had purposely placed myself to somehow manage my previously mentioned grief. I projected myself back into the real world, trying to remain outside of that madness. Working had helped bring a feeling of peace to my soul. By the time we started classes in channeling, I was no longer consumed by my sorrow, but rather taking steps to heal.

In my early twenties, I attended a séance at my parent's home. They had a friend in town and invited him to dinner. I, too, was invited. My younger sister still lived at home, so she was also present. After dinner, the conversation turned to a discussion of several passages in the Bible. The discussion was thoroughly enjoyable. I had never conversed with anyone who knew and understood the Bible as well as Frank did.

Imagine my shock when he asked my mother if she was ready for a séance. I had heard about this type of thing before. My church had taught me that it came from the stuff of the devil. For whatever reason, we all agreed to move forward with this suggestion. The psychic then closed his eyes. When he opened them, a woman's voice came out of his mouth. This energy knew of my fright and suggested that my little sister hold my hand as we continued. She (the woman he had contacted) answered the many questions we presented and gave us information that was so accurate my curiosity was peaked. This was a channeled session, although I didn't know it then.

At that time, I didn't pursue this modality any further, although I did indulge in an occasional reading by a psychic, just to see what they had to say. I was convinced of their accuracy regarding my current life yet questioned their predictions.

Nothing about spirituality frightens me anymore. I knew this was the direction I wanted to take once it was presented during my crisis of grief. My husband chooses not to believe as I do. However, he does not stand in my way as I shift and change. He knows I am happier than I have been in a long time.

During channeling classes, the instructor taught us a mantra to use for protection. After many years of this work, I have learned a great deal from several different teachers and have since dropped that practice. Now, I know I can set the intention that the channeling will come from pure white light. That light does not allow darkness to enter. There is always good and evil, but I prefer to stand in the light.

I mentioned in the previous chapter how I came to meet my Master Guide, Amadeus, and how I eventually learned who he was in relation to me. It is comforting to know that there is an energy on the Other Side who has chosen to guide me through this lifetime. Sometime in 2007, Amadeus spoke through me for the first time. He continues to be with me and, as a result, his messages still come to me to this day. As long as I am living, he will be my Master Guide. He will be there to teach, protect and help me move freely through the remainder of my journey.

He, and all the others who have come to be with me, have brought messages of self-improvement and enlightenment. Today, I am still learning how to be the best I can be. When I slip, this Team reminds me, and I jump back onto the path of spirituality and try to get on with the rest of my life. As they gently prod me in the right direction, they remind me that I am human. At times, I slip back into old habits, only to be brought back once more, lovingly, without judgment, into the light. If this sounds redundant, know that I will repeat it, as I frequently fall off course, only to be lifted back to the path I have chosen.

Just this week, I heard a message that I was to put a day's worth of my medication and vitamins in my purse and carry it with me. I smiled to myself, and then inadvertently found myself ignoring that thought. Not consciously aware that I was hearing from my Guides to follow their direction, I proceeded to close the bottle and put it away.

The following day, as it progressed, I became increasingly distraught. That morning, I had forgotten to take my medication, and it was affecting the palsy that is a part of my life. It became so bad I couldn't drive home. I called my husband and he lovingly brought me my forgotten medication.

Within half an hour of taking this little pill, my body settled down, and I realized that my Team had tried to protect me from my own forgetfulness the night before. Usually, I try so hard to listen, but the subtle way they guide me at times makes me forget to listen. Yes, that is another one of the flawed human parts of me.

I have made the decision to do a past life regression, so I can determine when this palsy entered my family's DNA. I am sure that, with some work, I will be able to conquer it, and it will not occur in my lineage again. It will also heal retrospectively so that none of my family members who have been afflicted with it in any lifetime will ever have to battle it again. The most wonderful part will be when I am finally able to toss the medicine bottle away!

I so enjoy bringing the messages I receive from my Guides and Others to the rest of the world. As you read this, I ask you to understand that the messages you receive are exactly what you need to hear on the day that you have chosen to hear them. I understand that before we are born into the life we are living this very day, we sit with a council of our Team and determine what we would prefer to work on in this lifetime. We learn lessons each time we reincarnate, and should we not learn all we are to learn, we work on those issues when we return to the other side of the veil. In this way, we have a master plan, but can make choices to follow it exactly or deviate somewhat.

By choosing this book, whether in paperback or the electronic version, it has come into your hands just at the exact right time on your journey. Between these pages, there are many things with which your soul wants a connection. Don't worry. This book is brought to you in Divine love and patience with the hope that you will glean satisfaction about who you are and the direction you will be taking as you walk the path in front of you.

I invite you, Dear Reader, to research and question each new idea that is presented in this book. Currently, I teach classes in Automatic Writing and Channeling, Spiritual Enlightenment Conversations, Children's Meditation, and Standing in Trust. The class genre may change, but the teacher within me will remain at peace with the messages I receive.

As a student and teacher, I implore you to always seek more advice when learning something new. If you don't question and confirm, doubt can creep into your belief system. Trust can easily fly out the window of your mind. I invite you to practice trust! Pick up another book, take another class, or surf the internet for answers to anything you question here or anywhere else. When you find a common thread that resonates with you, you may feel more at peace.

For myself, I wish to continue my writing, talking about love, and about releasing others from pain they have endured in this lifetime or in previous ones. This is my reality, and it is what makes me smile when I arise each morning to greet yet another day!

As you see, we have conscious choices. We do not have to mindlessly devour everything that comes across our life path.

Someone I met recently asked me if I would like to learn about a certain type of extraterrestrial. I could have seen it as a sign from my Guides to get involved. Yet, because I have the power to choose what I want in my life, I decided to investigate more and see what was being offered.

I googled the specific word the person had used and read the information. It didn't take long to realize I didn't want to become involved, then I closed the website. I have no plans to visit it again anytime soon. However, that option is still open for another time in the future if I so decide. For now, that door will remain closed.

As I continue to learn and decide what I wish for in my life, I know there are things I can consciously choose not to learn about. For the time being, I am not particularly interested in learning about extraterrestrial beings. I admit, I believe they do exist, and I choose to believe there is life on other planets. Perhaps one or more of my previous lifetimes took place in these other realms. Right now, I prefer to be here to teach the world about love; the love of self and of others. I am here to help to bring restoration to the earth plane and to bring healing to so many. I can freely choose what I want to do, and what I don't want to do. Should the subject of extraterrestrials one day become part of my journey, it will be at a time when I am able to welcome them. Currently, I have no time to ponder life on another planet as my plate is already quite full!

I am reiterating one more time; research carefully and always select what resonates with you. Do your homework. You have been blessed with an insight that gives you the ability to tell yourself yes or no. When you get an intense feeling that something is right, step up and enjoy the process of following your intuition. Alternately, when you sense something that is not in your best interest, don't hesitate to walk away.

I am Thor!

I come to you this day, Lovely One, to address the subject of this chapter.

Yes, I represent the Celtic God of thunder and lightning and the healing of the Earth. That is not all I am empowered to address. I am acutely aware of the movement in the Universe.

There are other dimensions, but you have rightly chosen not to address them at this time as a conscious choice. We are proud you have gotten the message to stay away from it for now. When the time comes that you need this information, it will be open to you. This subject could become all-consuming and we have plans to honor your path of teaching love of self.

I, too, am assisting with the writing of this book, and I am impressed with the way you address your audience regarding their choice of movement in their current lifetime. You are guiding them, and not force feeding them your personal beliefs. We all love that you encourage them to voice their preference on their personal journey.

They may think their path has been carved out before this incarnation and that they cannot participate in the process. That couldn't be further from the truth. The truth is that an alcoholic can choose outside help or continue to drink. A woman can choose to bring forth new life into the world or decide she wishes to depend on birth control. A homeless person may choose to live off the land, so to speak, or they can seek help that will bring them back to health and earning their own way in the world.

There are too many examples to leave here. Just know that we stand behind your gift to teach people about taking on only what resonates. Elect to study and believe what you wish and leave the rest.

Loving you, Thor.

CHAPTER IX

Past Life Relationship with Mozart

S even years of channeling the Spirit of Amadeus brought me to a new revelation. It happened while I was giving a presentation at a Holistic Faire. A young boy in the audience asked why Amadeus' sister was not as gifted as Amadeus had been. In response, Amadeus spoke. He revealed that he had blocked her energy.

During childhood in that lifetime, the children did not know about protecting themselves from someone intruding on their essence. What this young rascal did, was to interfere with the power of his multi-talented older sister so that she was unable to outshine him once he realized that she was writing music of her own. It started with him just hiding her music for which she was reprimanded by her parents for her carelessness. Later, he mastered the power of convincing his father that it was he that should bring fame to the family pointing out that his sister's talents were beginning to be overshadowed by his brilliance. His only goal was to gain fame and fortune for himself in that lifetime, and he needed to be sure she was not a threat to his mission.

If you read the history of this man, you will find that he was pompous and quite smitten with himself. As much as he enjoyed fame, he constantly hungered for more: more fame, more money and more women.

This is what I have read and researched about Amadeus. It has been documented by many, therefore I have no reason to discount this information. Nevertheless, that was in that lifetime. And this is now. I cannot hold any judgment on his past behavior. He has been reincarnated many times over to learn the lessons he had to learn. This has allowed him to remain on the Other Side, and to guide me along this current lifetime.

Following the exchange with the boy mentioned above, a man sitting in the back row asked Amadeus if he was the younger brother to the channel, meaning me, in that lifetime. Let me tell you, the moment I heard 'yes' in answer to his question, I panicked and abruptly lost my connection with Amadeus. In that instant, I did not feel worthy of holding that position back in that lifetime. How could I have been so talented and been as amazing as the articles I had read referring to Amadeus' older sister? I did not love me in that moment when it was being suggested that I was the infamous Nannerl, five years older than this entity I was currently channeling. After a moment, I looked directly at the man and said accusingly, "No one has ever asked me that question." It was rather amusing as the man was not actually asking me, Frances, he was asking Amadeus.

Realizing what I had just done, right in front of my audience, I quickly closed my eyes, and breathed a soft breath. When I opened my eyes once more, Amadeus was back with me. I realized then that he was the younger brother. My younger brother. Right then, I heard the message that he had come to assist me in this lifetime. He was there to help me achieve my life plan, and to heal the Karma between us. Without question, my energy told me that I had agreed to this treatment by Amadeus so that he would come into this lifetime to assist with my loving me and teaching it to you. Thus, I have ultimately forgiven him as you will come to hear later in this chapter.

Most of us return to the same circle of souls we circulated with during our past lives. Yet some remain on the Other Side, as Amadeus has, and continue to do their work from there. This means that the soul once known as Wolfgang Amadeus Mozart, as he chose to call himself in the 1700's, has achieved all he was meant to do here on Earth, and now resides permanently on the Other Side. He does however, have the option to choose to reincarnate should he decide he has missed something he wished to change. Healing past life Karma is crucial to moving forward in your current journey, and he is doing that now. He chose this lifetime to be with me in order to heal the wounds of our past life as the Mozart children. In this lifetime, I can stand in my own light. I am now able to accept spirituality and my gifts without the threat of death that has been a constant in many other lifetimes. Now, Amadeus can help me stand on the stage and speak my truth.

Even after I began meditation, automatic writing and channeling, I continued to visit other classes to observe other's channeling and to grow in my gifts. As I listened intently to the channel who was leading a class at the school one evening, messages were being given and received by everyone in the group. Surprisingly, as the instructor began to speak, he signaled to me and said that Amadeus was seeking forgiveness for blocking my energy during our lifetime together. This fellow channel related that Amadeus was standing nearby, with tears in his eyes, as he asked for this act of unconditional love to be granted by me. My Master Guide had gone to the teacher to have him relay this information to me.

"How would I accomplish this?" I pondered this predicament over the course of a few days, and eventually came to a very interesting conclusion. I would have my hypnotherapist lead me though a past life regression. It took some time for us to clear our schedules so that we could have a couple of hours to ourselves. In her office, I settled into the comfortable black recliner once more.

Christina gently guided me through the session. The hypnotherapist's voice had a cadence to it, which helped pull me into the vibration of relaxation and hypnosis. As I regressed, I went back into a lifetime in the 1700s. It was the period I had chosen before the session. There, I found myself as a nine-year-old little girl practicing her violin. We were in a grand house with highly polished wooden floors. There was a harpsicord in the drawing room and several musical instruments lined the bookcases. This was the room where Amadeus and I had learned to become multi-talented musicians.

Looking around, I saw my brother, Amadeus, practicing on his beloved harpsicord. He was four at that time. As exactly as described above, there were times that little prankster hid my music, so I could not practice my lessons. I was witnessing his devilish ways. When I told our parents, I couldn't find my music, they scolded me for being careless and naughty. They made me feel unloved, and imperfect. That continuing feeling of being unlovable that has plagued me throughout most of my lifetimes was again revealed. It has been a part of me starting many lifetimes ago. It occurs to me now that, when a child is constantly disciplined, their self-worth is attacked and their love of self-diminishes in their subconscious.

At that time, in that life, I felt Amadeus was mean for doing what he did. Regressing back to that point helped me to see that he was a prankster, and always laughing at my dilemma as I searched for the lost music. This mischief was what got me into trouble with our parents, and I was now supposed to forgive his actions.

I was brought forward by Christina who took me further back into that lifetime. Now I was twenty-three and married. We were in the concert hall, watching Amadeus perform on stage. He was brilliant in his delivery of the composition he had written. I felt envy that day. Then, the hypnotherapist pointed out that, even if I had not been in trouble because of my little brother, I could never have been on the stage with him. I was a woman. I was destined to be a wife and a mother. Society never would have supported me in my quest to perform music on that dais.

As we moved forward with the regression, I realized how easy it was to forgive my mischievous little brother. At four years old, he did not fully understand what he was doing when he hid my music. To him, it was just a fun little game that he was playing.

Now, on the Other Side, my brother from that lifetime was concerned about the impish behavior he had displayed as a young boy, or so I thought. Knowing we had already altered the energy between us, I knew that Amadeus would continue to assist me in this lifetime as I write, teach and learn my lessons. At that point, I felt we were done. I breathed in gratitude and breathed out sadness for what I could not accomplish hundreds of years ago, simply because I was a woman.

Tears stung my eyes as I realized that I lived then for love, and I now know my little brother loved me during our life together, and he continues to love me now. There are amazing revelations to the story between Amadeus and me. The rest of this narrative will be revealed later. I'll just say that this was not the only thing for which Amadeus was seeking forgiveness.

The regression was undeniably healing for me as it explained why Amadeus had chosen me to guide in this lifetime. I was no longer in question about the why and the ability for me to receive such a grand musician to choose to be with me now. It also assisted in the progress of Amadeus' soul as being forgiven meant he was being enabled to heal what Karma existed between the two of us and fulfill his promise to himself to watch over me and make my appearances in front of audiences filled with ease. So far, there have been dozens of small venues where I speak and channel. Who knows what the future has in store; I can't give predictions for myself as I am too close to the energy within me.

I did not set out with the intention to channel energy from the Other Side in this lifetime. However, channeling was embedded in my sub-conscious, and my life has subsequently followed the path that led me to this part of my journey. By conducting the energy of Amadeus and Others, I have been able to teach myself the great love and respect that I must show myself and to other people.

The messages brought forth in my writings have helped me find a sense of peace that settles deep within my solar-plexus. (The solar-plexus is represented in the chakra system as the third chakra from the bottom of the chakra system and is located behind the navel. It appears as the color yellow. The nerve endings here may give you a nervous or peaceful feeling. There are seven main energy centers, known as chakras, in the body and they run in a line up the spine. They each have a color assigned to them and a purpose.) This profound sense of serenity overshadows any feelings of calm I ever felt before. Now, I conduct sessions with others to assist with their healing by bringing forth messages from the Other Side. Currently, I am a psychic, a medium, a channel, spiritual coach, a hypnotherapist, and an author as well. These are all ways in which I can assist people with their recovery process.

Being psychic can be likened to entering a state of consciousness wherein one hears, feels, knows, smells or sees certain things within another person's energy field. It is having a deep knowledge about another person sitting next to me or halfway around the world. Do understand, if there is something you wish no one else to ever know, your energy reminds you to provide a barrier, so a psychic cannot enter the private place where you store that which is only of concern to you. Don't hang on to the belief that you can't visit a psychic because you think they might reveal all. You are the sole director of your life, and of what you allow or disallow.

A medium is one who receives messages from loved ones on the Other Side. I say loved ones because they love you when they are released from their earthly bodies. Many, from my paternal grandmother to my parents, to in-laws from both marriages, frequently send me love and wish they had given more love to me when they were here beside me on Earth. In the past, I desperately longed for the love they unconsciously withheld and now have the privilege of knowing it is there.

My grandmother's reaction was particularly harsh when she heard the news that I had been conceived. My father was forced to inform his mother that he wouldn't be able to send her money anymore, as his expenses were increasing. Sadly, my mother seemed to relish in letting me know many times over that my grandma had said she wished I hadn't been born at all. This grandma never loved me. While my siblings received birthday cards with two dollars tucked inside, I received none. Whenever she sent news she was visiting, there was tense scurrying by my mother to tidy the house. Out came the shrill side of my mother as she did what she despised. Also, the wooden spoon that was taken to our backsides to get the house in order for the pending visit vividly appeared. I dreaded grandma's arrival with her suitcases and latest husband (there were many 'grandpas' as my grandma had no luck in choosing men due to their demise or divorce).

Finally, one visit, she brought her new husband, Walter. Walter was a fun-loving character and seemed to not know about my grandma's distaste for me. He enjoyed teasing his wife's quiet little granddaughter, me. Shortly before their departure, he asked me when my birthday was. I told him, May 23rd and he said to watch the mail as he was going to remember that.

That very year and every year until his death some years later, I received a birthday card with two dollars in it just like all my siblings. From where she now resides, my grandma has asked forgiveness. I have peacefully forgiven her.

This feeling of being unloved came with a sense of knowing I had an idea of what I wished love to be and my grandma was incapable of expressing that in any way. I am aware of many people who came into my life during this incarnation who should have loved me with abandon yet did not. Both of my mothers-in-law, my ex-husband and my current husband's father have come through during sessions with a medium to express their love for me and their regret for not having given me all the love they could when they were physically with me. Their withholding love was part of my journey with them as I fought my battle to love the me in me.

My forgiveness of their non-action is always granted sometime after an incident has been revealed. Forgiving transgressions against me makes *me* feel better. I do care if those who have passed on also feel better, but it is the good feelings within *me* that make forgiveness a necessary choice. I am able to forgive someone still residing on Earth, or one who has crossed into the light. It doesn't matter where the energy of the person is connected, it matters that my forgiveness frees me of those burdens. Ultimately, upon choosing to forgive, they are also able to heal, whether they are here physically or not.

Channeling is about making a conscious choice to take automatic writing to the next level. It is where Ego moves aside to leave space for another entity to enter your field and speak through you. Not everyone wishes to attain this level. At times, as a novice channel, you may feel a strange scratchiness in your throat.

During one of the classes, my teacher provided the following explanation, and I found myself comforted by this new information. She said that you may feel the need to cough or yawn during a guided meditation for others, or even while doing a quiet meditation if you are working alone. These are signs that you are being prepared to bring in an entity from the Other Side. This is not always the case but, as I began to learn to channel, my yawns were extremely pronounced, and quite frequent. I tried to hide them during class-guided meditations. It felt rude to yawn (self-judgment before self-love). However, it's quite normal.

It is for you to decide if you wish to choose this path. If so, you may gravitate towards channeling verbally for others, or you may decide to only write with your Team. You might choose neither one of these modalities, or both. Whatever you choose, don't forget that you are loved unconditionally.

It is I, Amadeus, Sweet One.

How very brave you were to do the regression in the hopes of sending me the forgiveness I asked for that night in the class when I visited your instructor. Yes, Sweet One. That was the very thing missing when reviewing my lifetime with you as my sister, Nannerl, officially named Maria Anna.

We have had other lifetimes together, but that was the one I carried with me as I had been unseemingly cruel. (Unseemingly is not a word I even know, although I have researched it and learned to use this new word! They teach me all

the time about many things and this is just one of them. This is an example of them being part of this missive.) *Not just with hiding your music, but with other things. I knew you could never travel like I did because of the era in which we lived, and how they treated women then. I blocked some of your energy so that you would not outshine me. I needed the help of our father to bring me into the limelight. If he continued to think of you as the gifted one, I would not have gained the respect I longed for. When you lost some of your hold over him, there was room for me to thrive as I needed.*

I am here to assist you in any way I can because, in this lifetime, you can bring forth your gifts for all to know, and to hear them applaud you.

I thank you for following your instincts and forgiving me for my blunder. Even as you thought the forgiveness was solely for the mischief, it carried over into some other outlandish deeds. I was selfish at the time. As I witness the world listen to and play my music, I know that we had an agreement, before we incarnated together in the 1700s, that I should write and play. It does not excuse any of my unsavory behavior. We can now see it as lessons learned then and lessons completed now.

Go in love, light and laughter, Amadeus.

I see, through this message, that although the hypnotherapist and I worked on the four-year-old mischief, it had functioned much further and quite differently than either of us expected. Perhaps with another hour, we would have uncovered the rest of the story, but forgiveness is pure and thorough. You only need to say, "I forgive" once. There is no need to revisit any other issue with the soul in question. The energy of forgiveness is already in the energy of the Universe and it reverberates wherever it needs to travel.

I feel much lighter knowing what I now know about the lifetime I shared with Amadeus. I, too, knew some of the unsavory ways of his adulthood, but he was working with what he knew at the time, and with what his soul needed to bring about the amazing music that stays forever in the hearts of those who hear it. I listen at home, and in the car, along with many of the concertos created by others through the centuries.

One Saturday, during a talk at a Holistic Faire, Amadeus was asked about his favorite composition. He said that he did not favor any of his work over anyone else's. He told his audience, at that time, that since his departure from the earth plane there have been countless musical geniuses who have composed extraordinary melodies. At one point, he mentioned Michael Jackson as one who resides among the greatest musicians who has ever lived. He has learned to be humble with his work where he now resides, and Ego no longer commands his soul.

CHAPTER X

Energy of Past Lives Affecting Current Life

Often, I sit in counsel with a client who has personal issues with someone who has crossed their path. Let's say, for example, that it is a co-worker, someone who is new to the office. Just imagine the new employee entering the space where you spend most of your waking hours and finding their energy drastically puts you off. They call me for a session and we begin to work through the dilemma. More than likely the newbie is innocent and unaware of the disruptive vibration they are bringing into the work place.

You see, this unwanted energy may have to do with past life unresolved issues. Do I suggest my client confront them with this information? Absolutely not! If the person in question is not spiritually-minded, they will probably assume my client is mentally incompetent and maybe even report him/her to the Human Resources Department on harassment charges. They also might be offended if they know they are causing a disruption, and that they are disliked in the office. This would add further negativity to an already unpleasant environment.

To solve this type of problem, we have options here on Earth. One can sit in silence, surrounding the scene at work with white light and forgiveness, and hold the vision until the light changes to a soft pink that encompasses the room, and becomes a blanket of love. My gentle guidance could assist in this recovery, if warranted.

The offended party could also surround themselves with a metal or plexiglass shield, decorated or not, and the newbie's energy would not be able to pass through the shield and offend.

Another option is to conduct a past-life regression with the client and try to get to the actual root of the problem. This will depend on the person going into hypnosis, their comfort with a session of this type, and how deeply rooted the problem has become.

Usually with just one session, we can uncover what happened in that past life to bring about this emotional reaction. Once we know, it is easily released by simply understanding that it has nothing to do with the actual incarnated soul.

During subsequent sessions, we discover ways to continue to purge the incident from the subconscious mind, bring it into the present and deal with its consequences. The example of the episode in the workplace would then solve itself with the simple act of forgiving the coworker for their disruptive energy and its subsequent negative effects. The client is then able to process the energy into a positive force and move forward. Notice there does not have to be a verbal face to face reconciliation. The person doing the forgiving simply puts the absolution out into the Universe. This works for the good of the client and will bring about a positive change in the working environment due to a new understanding that was retrieved during the session.

We practice this method out of love. It does no one any good to be distraught over an uncomfortable situation in the workplace, or anywhere else, when it can so easily be rectified. One must be ready to change the energy to place a call to me in the first place, so they are prepared to do the work involved.

I ask you to revisit some of the more unnerving situations you have found yourself in during this lifetime. See if you can recognize that this could have come from past life energy, and how you may have already worked through it.

This past-life recognition does not always have to be due to ill-laden Karma. I think of the many people I have met and felt an immediate recognition of them even though we had never met in this lifetime. It seems to happen often in my spiritual community, and I believe it must be due to the like-minded seeking a place of community and of their connectedness to the soul energy we all carry.

It immediately reminds me of a young man in his early twenties who volunteered for several months at a metaphysical school where I taught meditation, automatic writing and channeling. I called him Sebastian. That was not his name in this lifetime, but for me, the energy of this young man's soul shouted, "Sebastian". I tried many times and, try as I might, to this day I still stop everything and clearly ponder his correct name. He is now a friend of mine. After more than three years, I began writing an email to him and as I pulled up the addresses on my email list, his name was not there ... or was it? Yes, of course it was there, and it was not Sebastian! His name in this lifetime is completely different but does start with an 'S'.

I also would love to tell you about another beloved student and good friend of mine. Her name is Elizabeth. We were teacher and student. Yet, as months passed, I could not get the name Barbara out of my mind. Clearly, I could get it out of my mouth, and each time it spewed forth, we laughed in mutual understanding that there was something we might need to explore regarding our past lives together. I know I was happy in that past life because I enjoyed her energy from the moment we met. I love her laughter! Had our relationship been difficult in our past life together, that unfavorable energy would have remained, and we would have been at odds. Neither of us would know exactly why, but we would not be able to maintain a relationship of joy.

It became such an embarrassment in class that I would look at her, stop for a moment, think Barbara, and finally say Elizabeth. Our connection is strong and, although she has moved away, we remain friends. She is still Barbara/Elizabeth to me in this lifetime.

You might wish, at some point, to consider your relationships with some of the people in your current or past life during this incarnation. Is there anyone you recognize readily as a past life connection? Are there some you wonder about now that this issue is right in front of you? Play with the concept. Research the information here and try to contemplate why a certain person does not resonate with you, or why someone else makes you feel comfortable in a way that others cannot. Have some fun with it. After all, this life is meant to be fun and there should be some pleasure contained within its lessons.

The more I read and dig into the practice of Hypnotherapy, the more informed and intrigued I become. It gradually became apparent why these meetings would begin so awkwardly and then transform into something positive. I will share with you the concept of what I have learned.

I have memories in my lifetime of meeting a person and immediately disliking them. I did not wish to engage them in conversation in any way whatsoever. I always wondered about this initial bad feeling and pondered why so many of these souls I met later were then able to become quite close to me.

Let's begin with meeting a person I did not appreciate on our first encounter. Who was he to me in a past incarnation? Perhaps we were on opposing sides on the battlefield. Maybe he was protecting his king's beliefs, and I was doing the same for mine. Were they really our own beliefs, or were we mere puppets acting in accordance with the kingdoms into which we had both been born? That is the underlying question here.

As we charged into battle, and this soul thrust his sword between my ribs and straight into my heart, my last memory of his energy was my death. His victory was my loss. I never returned to my sweetheart to marry and raise a family. I was lost to that life forever.

Moving forward many lifetimes, my first sense of his energy upon meeting him in this incarnation was that brief memory cloaked in my subconscious mind. As time progressed, my sub-conscious mind processed the past lifetime energy and empowered me to forgive him for the death scene.

We were at war, and that was what we did. Problem solved. Now, I was able to move forward with this relationship on any level I chose.

There is another incident I would love to tell you about. I was taking a seminar on hypnotherapy and became rather intrigued when we began the past life regression section! As the instructor began her discourse, leading us into the process of regression, I let myself drift under her spell. She realized I was gone and used me as her volunteer for the exercise.

The instructor asked me questions and guided my trip. The following story is an account of what transpired as she led me through that lifetime.

I was back in the 'ole west'. I was a cowboy tying my horse to the hitchin' post. I wandered into the saloon for a beer to sooth my dry and dusty throat. While there, I inquired about a job.

Later, as I meandered down the road, I entered the mercantile and was hired to load sacks of wheat and other grains onto farmers' wagons. I toiled in the sun and took short breaks in the shade of the cottonwood tree. That was the only place to be comfortable.

Life in the dusty little town was bearable, and I put down roots. I met and married the town widow. Her family and the townspeople were the only guests present at the ceremony. I had left behind all contacts and familiar ties when I moved to my new settlement.

The instructor finally asked where I was when I took my last breath in that lifetime, and exactly how I had died. I was quite surprised to reach this point because it was clear that I had been poisoned by my wife. Again, she was back in her place of prominence, as the town widow. My body was laid out for viewing on the kitchen table, as was the custom. The next day I was buried in a wooden box which was nailed shut and interred where my body would rest forevermore.

As she brought me gently and slowly out of my hypnotic state, my instructor queried me about any knowledge I might have about the characters who played a part in that lifetime.

Then, I divulged that the brother of the woman I married is my current husband! There is one man connected to my circle of friends and family with whom I prefer not to converse with or be in touch with. It appears that his soul energy was the same energy of the wife who poisoned me in that previous life.

My first reaction upon reviewing that life was to feel validated for not being fond of the man I have always avoided. Yet, after a few days of pondering the situation, I also wondered what I may have done to this woman/man that was so bad, that they had purposely poisoned me.

Was I a drinker and rabble-rouser causing embarrassment for her in the town? Or, did I have a wandering eye? Perhaps I was not an abundant provider and she wished to support only herself with whatever it was she had done before I came along.

While I could do another regression, and delve further into that situation to learn more, it does not interest me enough to find out. A more interesting source of intrigue is wondering what I will feel or think the next time this person comes into my circle. How will I feel then? In preparation, I put a white light around the memory of the regression and sat with it until the pink blanket appeared. Hopefully, we should find ourselves with good energy when we are together again as the soul has been forgiven its transgression.

It is I, Amadeus, Dear One.

I have come to sit with you as you digest what you have just written. You remember the day of this regression concerning a current life relationship and you ponder why you were plucked from the Universe at the hands of your supposed beloved wife.

As you stated, the reasons do not matter in this lifetime. What does matter is the lessons that were learned in that lifetime. Whatever it was, it was meant to be, and you were meant to cross into the light in the very way that you did.

As always, you made your agreements before you came into that lifetime and there were lessons to be learned. As they were understood, you were released to move forward into the Light and return to the Source to examine what had been discovered and what still needed to be worked on.

In subsequent lifetimes, those things you still needed to learn were again presented to you. I am very proud of you, as you have conquered those lessons you needed to progress and propel you into the life you are currently living.

It is in this lifetime you have been given new lessons. One was to lose someone immensely dear to your heart and live through the realization that he is only a whisper away. You are also here to grasp the tenants of your spirituality and live by them.

We are aware of those that you struggled with, and are celebrating here with Source, the accomplishments that have been crucial to you. We are also here to assist you in any way that we are able and allowed to do. We wish to make your life exactly what you want it to be.

You have many years left of good strong health to provide all you can with your gifts of advice, healing, connection with Spirit and their personal regressions. It is what you have come to do, along with living the loving life you have created with family and with friends. Keep your candle burning brightly so that all can find your light in the world.

You are loved immeasurably by all of us here, and so many there that you don't even know where this writing is coming from. You trust us implicitly and yet you are quiet with Ego and wish to be a beacon in the shadows. We regret to inform you that your light is shining much too brightly for you to hide and you will soon understand what we are saying.

Stay true to self, filled with the love you have taught unto you, and wish to teach unto others.

Go, Dear One in love, light and laughter for eternity!

Lovingly, Amadeus.

CHAPTER XI

Learning of Love of Self

This morning, I requested that my Guides and Others be patient with me during meditation. I wanted a moment to quiet my mind before they began their messages. I felt the need to bask in the silence as the day began to unfold around me. Yes, I can make requests of Spirit, and they will honor my needs. You have the power to direct how much or how little they can chat with you, and when you wish for them to participate in your day and in decisions for your life. If it is late at night and you wish to sleep, let them know, "Save it for the morning."

Once I was thoroughly relaxed and at peace, I invited them to chat with me about the progress of this book. The passage below had been transcribed directly from my journal. I keep it beside me during meditations to capture the messages on paper, thus giving me something with which to refer when I need to review a directive they may have given me at any given time. I prefer to date my journal entries so that there is a continuum of their sage advice.

It is I, Amadeus. Good morning, Sweet One!

You have a great start on your book. Remember it is just a first draft and may be changed at any time by you, or by us. Keep in mind that this is being given to the world through you from us. We are assisting you so that it flows and is done in a much shorter time than your last book. You need to continue to write each day and reveal your writings.

We so enjoy taking time out of our day to work with you. That is said with tongue in cheek as there is no time here on the Other Side. This is a concept that is difficult for mankind to wrap their heads around. There is really no time on Earth either, but humans work so much better when they can look at a clock.

You sleep and rise at certain times, and make sure you are on time for the meetings you undoubtedly set for yourselves to put pressure into your lives. Some humans choose to never be on time. They are usually considered self-centered as the others wait for the missing member of the group. Many of you pass judgment on this soul, even though you wait for

***them. It is totally fine with us as we understand
you are human beings, living with the soul who
chose to incarnate as you in this lifetime. You
are learning to stop this judgment and step into
discernment.***

***Continue to teach all who will listen to
stop judging others. Allow these late comers
to arrive peacefully feeling no pressure from
you or the others. Share your confidence and
proceed in joy.***

Love, Amadeus

When I know I am truly in the flow of the channeling on
paper, I realize the handwriting has changed and I, who have
respectable handwriting, can barely read what has been scrawled
upon the journal page.

Each of the entities that come through me with messages on
paper, have distinct penmanship. Amadeus's handwriting has
wiggly large letters and he uses my pen in a wild way reminiscent
of the mischievous ways of his four-year-old self. Thor's script
is so big and bold that it fills the page with only about twenty
words, yet the touch on paper is as light as a feather.

The latest I have written with are Archangel Gabriel and
Archangel Metatron. Their handwriting is similar to each other's
and controlled. The letters are large and written straight up and
down. They're quite different than any of the others. The female
energy of Justine, Mother Theresa and the fairy, Mathilda (with an
'h'), on the other hand, write a little bit more like my own hand. Often,
all of them use expressions I find unfamiliar in my spoken word.

Loving the Me in Me

These entities introduce themselves when I write, all have affectionate names for me, and end with a loving salutation. Not all Guides or other energies introduce themselves. Many energies that I have heard from do give introductions of themselves, but I have also listened to those who are just representing a singular entity, or a conglomerate from the Universe and choose not to identify with a name. There is no right or wrong here. It is what it is, and we must accept them the way they choose to come to us as they write with us. Always know that we remain in control.

My Team surrounds me with a deep sense of peacefulness that I have searched for in many lifetimes. It is a blessing to feel their love surrounding me as I sit here gazing out at the greenbelt behind my current home. The blue sky, the tall trees, a slight breeze blowing the leaves and palm fronds. Perfection meets the day.

This is how I spend my mornings, as often as possible. I type away at this manuscript staring off into this wonderment, knowing I am exactly where I am supposed to be on this day, now and in this moment. I hope this description is something you can sink into and surround yourself with just by reading these lines.

As I write this, I can't help but think of all the souls who do not live as I do. I have seen the poverty, squalid living conditions and distended bellies of those without food. I have seen the immigrants who have been forced from their countries by war. My heart is with them. I am working with all the energy I possess to teach the world of love of self which will, in turn, bring love to those who need a hand, a warm hug, a sweet hello with a smile on my face. I do not expect everyone else to do something I cannot do myself. I am working for the multitudes who will be healed when the fighting and lack of caring ends. It is my life's work to heal the world to the best of my ability in this lifetime.

There are many ways to feel and know love. It can come in the form of a warm hug from family or friends. Love can also be felt when an entity from the Other Side brings their energy into your personal energy field. You feel this love with a sweeping emotion felt inside the heart and solar plexus chakras.

Love can also be felt when you catch the twinkle in a baby's eye as they meet you each time you enter their sphere. Currently, I experience that feeling more and more often with the new little ones being welcomed into our family as it stretches and grows. Or, love can be a simple hello and a smile to someone who may be homeless and has been mostly overlooked due to fear and ignorance of their predicament, passing judgment on a situation they know nothing about. It may have been days or weeks since anyone has spoken to this homeless soul, and they are aware they are being dejected. Thus, a single morsel of attention makes them feel more alive than before the words were spoken to them.

I have gleaned such joy from complementing strangers on their great haircut, lovely tattoo, beautiful dress, etc. When their face lights up with pleasure, it warms my heart. I know that I have made a difference in their life for that moment and each time they remember how good it made them feel. I used to live in my solitude, not thinking of giving back in this small way. Now I know it has become so easy to live with others and brings joy to each of us.

Each day, I awaken to greet a new vibration. A new chapter in my life begins with the rising of the sun as I embark on a new day. Every sunrise brings an opportunity to leave the past behind and move forward in untold joy! I am in gratitude to be here, and to be able to do so many fascinating things.

I count my blessings daily. I review them in my mind and think about the possibilities the ensuing day might bring. There are always going to be the pitfalls in life, but the magic outweighs these losses, or failures if you wish to call them that. Nothing can be counted as a loss or a failure if you understand that each step backwards is also a lesson learned. Your personal growth stems from these amazing times that unfold each day without you having any idea of the outcome.

It wasn't always this way. There was a time when I felt lost, cheated somehow out of what I did not have. I was focused on what I lacked, clouding the infinite possibilities that lay before me. It took self-love for me to become conscious of the gifts that are mine. I learned to stop wallowing in pity. It was pointless wondering why someone else could live in grandeur and I could not. It was a waste of time pondering the fact that they had the most beautiful wardrobe while I shopped in less expensive stores. Those Capezio shoes from high school are but one example! So many had so many more material things than I did. Self-love brought about an understanding that all the material goods were not what mattered. What mattered was love. It brought me to a heightened awareness that I had all I needed. I can now enjoy family, friends and entities and look forward to their next visitation without wishing I had more money, more love, more respect, more, more, more.

The laughter ringing through the house as the family gathers together, or when good friends call to chat, makes me realize I have always been loved. The expression of love is different with each person and situation. Earlier in my life, love had eluded me as I did not know exactly what it was I sought. I had to consciously experience it in this lifetime to realize it had, in fact, always been there. My parents did love me in their own way. My friends thought loving thoughts about me, but they did not express them in so many words. Like the red slippers on Dorothy's feet in the "Wizard of Oz", they were there all the time. She simply needed to see them for what they were, click the heels together and be transported back to where she belonged. And so, did I.

Love of self has brought more love to surround me than I ever thought possible. It brings with it a sense of profound contentment with what I have so that it is not necessary to covet what others have, but instead I am able to relish what is in my life at any given moment.

If you recognize this in yourself, proceed to the mirror. Look deep into your eyes. "The eyes are the mirror to your soul," it is said. This idiom is reiterated by Amadeus throughout many presentations to his audience. Believe this. Look into your own eyes and say, "I love me." You may feel ridiculous as you utter the words, "I love me." "What do you think you are doing?" you ask. Yes, that is exactly the way it begins. If you do not yet love the 'you' in you, you will feel emotions ranging from absurd to devastation. Who cares? No judgment here! It takes a great deal of practice before this exercise begins to feel right. At least, that is the way it was for me and for others I have guided.

There is nothing easy about learning this love by looking in a mirror. It is a heart-wrenching process. You must go through many steps from the first attempt to the time when the task has been accomplished. You will remember atrocities that were hurled against your very body, mind and soul. You may wail to ease the pain. It is a painful process and yet, one day you will begin to smile, giggle and finally shout to no one but you; I love myself! I love the 'me' in me!

Each soul arrives at the realization of self-love when the time is right for them. I ask my readers that you seek to find out when that time might be right for you. If you never practice looking in the mirror, or trying to fall back in love with you, you may never come to know that feeling of immeasurable joy! Once you have attained this level of elation, everything you undertake flows so much more easily and smoothly than you ever imagined. As Amadeus has taught me, when we know how to love ourselves, it emanates to others. This love then needs to circle the Earth and bring healing to its core.

There is a way to love you gently and completely without letting Ego soar out of control. You are not loving you above all others. You are not loving you to prove to anyone but yourself that you are perfection. This is not a boastful love, it is a sincere and confident love of the energy you hold within your body.

This is the love you were born with, and you deserve to feel its presence. It's peace. Once you have achieved this love, you may notice tears trickling down your cheeks. Joyous tears of a new-found bliss that is YOU! Others in your life may notice a change in you and comment. There will be some energies that gravitate towards you, as they recognize the beauty radiating from your soul. Take all this admiration in your stride. You won't become boastful or obnoxious, you will become the calm, patient you who has been waiting to shine their light!

> *It is Justine. I am excited to sit with you, Dearest One.*
>
> *It is always such a delight to be able to speak with you during your meditation mornings. You*

have come so far with this love of self that I am moved to tell you of my love for you. I, too, have been with you in other lifetimes. You were never so sure of yourself in the past or as content as you are now. It is so beautiful to know how much you care about others and wish to help them heal their pain in their current lifetime.

You would not be so determined to help others had you not come to this place of love. As we work with you and the Guides of those you are working with, we can bring them to the same love and peace that you have achieved. You will take this energy with you when you leave the Earth at the predisposed time. When you, and all who learn to love themselves this way, return in your next incarnation, you will bring this love of self with you.

It is with this energy of love that healing this planet will be made possible, as is dictated in your contract, it will transpire.

It is my privilege to bring my love to this project and assist you in any way I am directed by the energy here on the Other Side. Go now, Sweet One, in love of self and others and enjoy your days as they unfold before you.

In love, Justine

CHAPTER XII

Healing with Sound

T oday another gentle breeze weaves its way onto my
patio and moves the wind chimes gently so that the
sounds are sweet and caress my soul with reverberation of music.

Six years ago, we found ourselves in a townhouse after the
sale of our home. On the first night of a Santa Ana wind, the
neighbor came knocking. It appeared that these chimes were
keeping his young daughter awake with their not so gentle
crashing noise. Respectfully, we took them from their location
at the edge of the small patio and placed them in the garage. For
the time we lived in Anaheim Hills these chimes were hushed.
They had been silent, until now in our new yard.

(A Santa Ana wind typically occurs in Southern California
during the fall and winter months when it becomes unseasonably

warm. Depending on the severity, they can be gentle or uproot trees. They can ignite fires in the dry tinder of the hills just by moving the grasses to and fro. We respect these winds and follow their directives. Originally known as San Tana; Devil Winds, time and slurring of the words brought us to Santa Ana Winds.)

The chimes had hung on our porch in the backyard of our home in the City of Orange located in Orange County, for about fifteen years prior to our move from our oversized home to a smaller place. With a house, a yard and plenty of space, they were not bothersome to anyone.

Gleefully, on this day in mention, I returned the chimes, with my husband's help, to their proper use on our patio at our new home in Tustin the very day before the Santa Ana winds visited us. They crashed and banged some, but in this new abode with a beautiful green belt behind it, there was no knocking on our door. As the winds quieted their rage, the music soothed my soul.

The magical sound of these chimes heard during my meditation this morning as I sat in my back yard, brought me to the memory of the first time I meditated with Gabriel Aumnow as he played his crystal bowls. To me, there was nothing like this original meditation with him. For an hour I laid on the hard floor of the room we were in, not noticing the creaks wracking my body. It was so gentle and so soothing that I drifted off to the darkness that is the part of my meditations when the sub-conscious mind takes over the conscious mind.

If you talk to anyone who leads a guided meditation and ask what happens when you seem to fall asleep, they will tell you that even though you missed the words or the music, you still received the message you were meant to receive. The lesson is still embedded in your sub-conscious mind to be retrieved at a later date or to just resonate with you as you move deliberately through the day.

After my second meditation with Gabriel and his crystal bowls, another person lying on the floor began to question how he had learned to play them; thus, a loving communication ensued.

Gabriel explained how the bowls were made and that each size of the instruments held a different vibration. As he played them, their sound blended with the music of the next one and a soothing composition was born. The calming effect it had on my soul began a new journey into the world of music which was already so familiar to me.

Is this the soothing reverberation from that lifetime with Wolfgang Amadeus Mozart? I don't even have to check with him as I know soundly, just as I know my own name is Frances in this lifetime, that this is true.

The next occasion, as I lay on my newly purchased mat in the room with Gabriel, I drifted softly off into this world of sound. I began to notice which parts of his display in front of him resonated better with me than others. The sound of the rattle that he shook near the end intrigued me and reminded me of a lifetime where American Indians shook their rattles and created the same sound. It felt like coming home.

The following week, on Tuesday, I wandered through the day with a new sensation settling itself into my very being. I began to question the feeling. Was I feeling depressed? "*No*," came the answer in my head. "*You have been depressed before and would recognize the sensation. You are at peace, Dear One. Music in most forms has soothing properties. You have*

played instruments in other lifetimes. This current existence you chose to sing. Bask in the joy you brought to your soul when you sang as a child and sing more often."

I felt blessed as the sounds from Gabriel's crystal bowls brought about a therapy for my soul. It took me back to the church with its hymns I sang in childhood and back to the high school chorus where I, an alto, sang in front of the audience. This is where my voice blended with the entire choral group to bring healing sounds to all who listened.

As a child, I didn't know of these soothing properties of music. I just knew that they made me happy as I heard the music and joyously sang the words. As an adult, I have learned that I have been blessed to be a healer in many forms and singing is just one small part of that healing power.

Peace. Bliss. Feelings I did not know were possible. Learning the love of me has brought elation to my heart and I long to share this with the world and bring them, each in some small way, into this vibration.

There are times when I get irritated, anxious or worried. I am, after all, human. Now though, when I stop and sit in stillness, I can bring that feeling of love and peace back into my heart and solar plexus.

I want to take a moment and talk with you about why I left the church I grew up in. I grew away from the church when I realized that I was being asked to fear God. I did not come to this decision lightly. It took many years of examination of my emotions regarding my church. To me, God is loving, giving, caring and gracious. The energy of Source, as I also refer to it often, brings such pleasant emotions as it soothes the soul. I feel that we are all part of that energy and can actually connect as God/Source energy.

Another part of the church I disagree with is the lavish buildings built with the tithing of the congregation. That money would be so much better spent feeding the masses and doing the work they propose they are committed to.

This is true of most churches and religions. I have found that there are some ministries in the community that have simple buildings and grounds and use their funds to do what they are best at doing, helping others grow and thrive. I may choose one day to sit in their congregation.

January 27, 2015 – It is I, Amadeus Dear One.

You sit in meditation for the silence. You sit in Crystal Bowl Meditation for the stillness brought to you by the oneness of the music. The gentle sounds reverberate through your energy field and bring you peace.

Some people find the sounds too much for them as they weave their way about the room. The energy can be disruptive to those not in sync with its vibrations. Not so for you. It is like coming home for you. You have played instruments or sung songs in all of your lifetimes. Even the one as the woman with the vegetable cart many lifetimes ago, you whistled while you toiled.

(I did a past life visitation and saw myself at a vegetable cart where I was crouched down giving a reading to another woman.)

> ***Music is great therapy for the soul. It brings light to all things. We wish for you to go inside and bring the child in you out to play and to sing. Find yourself in this peace again and again and wrap yourself in its love vibration. This, too, is a part of loving the 'you' in you.***
>
> ***Loving you, Amadeus.***

CHAPTER XIII

The Energy of the Earth Loving Me

The Santa Ana winds are blowing again today as I look outside of my door, reminding me of the strength of nature. How incredibly small and powerless mankind can be at the hands of Mother Nature. I believe I am loved by the energy of the Earth. Have you ever allowed yourself to sit with nature and ponder that thought? Often, I have been in awe of the beauty of the Earth but have not, until just now, considered it quite this way. Learning to love me is a lesson in loving others, nature and being in gratitude for all that is.

Driving up the California coastline, escaping from the mundane or hustle bustle of life in Orange County, I have stopped to linger on the sandy beach and watched as the waves gently lapped the shore. I have also been to the craggy coastlines of Northern California and watched as the waves pounded the rocks, throwing their spray into my face. The ocean has been known to cover islands, bring homes tumbling into the water and wipe out hundreds of people when a Tsunami roars onto shore after being awakened by an earthquake deep within the Earth itself. Yet, the same oceans draw in children and adults to frolic in its wake on sandy beaches and send fishermen over its unpredictable surface to bring their bounty to shore. Powerful destruction or supporting joy and feeding mankind.

At times, I visit the desert to embrace family living there and the energy is unmistakably moving. There is an energy in the desert that calls for calm and meditative contemplation.

Each year, I watch reports about violent storms, known as hurricanes or tornadoes, as they devour towns across America. They gather speed and tear indiscriminately through cities and countryside, destroying everything in their path! Along with the strength of their winds, they also bring intense rains that are almost a mockery to those already huddled in fear in basements or lying in the rubble of their homes.

When there is a flood, rivers break their banks and bring even more devastation to the ravaged Earth. This does not feel much like this planet is loving me and, yet, the forces of nature are what formed the mountains and the valleys and continue to form and reform the surface of the Earth. My eyes come to rest in gratitude regaling in their beauty and majesty and it brings me peace.

Other times, rain does not come, and the rivers, lakes and streams dry up. The droughts wreak havoc upon crops. As a result, food prices soar, leaving some people to scrounge for nourishment. It is during these times I question why I choose to believe that this is a form of love. Love is a great teacher, and with drought comes the lesson to use all the Earth's gifts lovingly and sparingly, bowing to its power.

In winter, the rain turns to freezing snow. Blizzards bring heavy weight to the branches of trees, pulling them to the ground and yanking power lines from their perches, leaving homes without electricity for light and warmth. We have all heard stories of the destruction caused by the snow as it piles on the roofs of homes or buildings, causing complete collapse and shattered window panes. Then, as the snow melts, sink holes appear. Yes, I find love in the winter too, as the snow becomes a winter wonderland and winter sports fill the days of so many. As the spring comes and the snow in the mountains melts, it nourishes the land and fills the lakes and rivers with the water so necessary for the next season to grow its crops, feed its people, and perpetuate mankind.

There are also moments when earthquakes rattle below the ground's surface. They, too, bring devastation. Buildings collapse, bridges are split in two and homes are destroyed. The Earth rumbles inside and volcanoes become active, spewing ash and lava for miles, opening the ground to swallow cars and anything else in its wake. Occupants are evacuated and then find themselves homeless. The surface of this planet is ever-changing with the love of a new beginning, a new lesson learned.

Let us not forget the ravaging fires that consume so much foliage and displace so many animals, birds and people as they tear through habitats day and night. Buildings and homes can burn to the ground, leaving entire lifetime memories in ashes. Yet, nature also has a way of providing fire to clear undergrowth to make way for the newness that will sprout and cover the area once more. Fire, when contained properly, brings warmth and a hearth with which to prepare the meals for the people of the Earth.

The cycles of the Earth bring devastation to some, but the coming together of the community and the multitudes makes us realize there is change and we are mere visitors who cannot claim to control all that has been given to us by the energies we seek to know. We rely on each other for protection and companionship to clear, rebuild and rebirth what has been torn down; loving each other in times of need. Spreading the love of self and others is what I write and teach about.

I continue to believe the energy of the Earth loves me. The rain that sometimes gently cleanses the atmosphere of dust particles, and makes flowers, trees and grasses grow is a blessing to us all. It washes everything clean, and a sparkle of love shines through. Moderation is the key here. This is a time when crops grow to feed the people living on its surface. A time of replenishment and plenty.

The warmth of the sun and the rain assist the trees and plants as they grow giving all of us a gift of beauty. Imagine the landscape without the glory of the meadows, the forests, the deserts, and grassy hillsides. We have all seen photos of other planets, devoid of the love we have of the landscape which pleases our eyes; bringing calm to our lives most days, supplying us with provisions for survival.

During guided meditation with my class or my clients, I always have them ground themselves to Mother Earth, as I wrote in an earlier chapter. By doing this through the root chakra, they are invited to hand back all the negative energy in their personal field to Gaia through this grounding cord. Gaia will then absorb all that negativity and transmute it into positive forces and return it to their bodies. Yes, the Earth loves me and you. There are other ways to ground. Walk on the Earth barefoot ten or so minutes a day, spend time in nature without distraction, or hug a tree! In my class, we use the grounding technique described above. There is a general recommendation for all of us to take off our shoes and spend 10-15 minutes per day with bare feet in the garden, grass or soil "grounding" to the Universe itself. It is with caution I make my way around this Earth. I avoid the crashing waves if they come too close. I hunker down when the wind and rain begin to rage; I wait for it to subside before venturing out. I have chosen not to live near active or inactive volcanoes, yet here I am, in Southern California where earthquakes jolt me out sleep at times during the night or sway the coffee in my cup. *"What's up with that?"* I ask myself.

There can be no escaping nature's twists and turns. It keeps me focused. I realize I am not the complete energy of all that is. Nature teaches me respect. With that I can feel its love. If it were not for nature, the very world as we know it today would not exist; no trees, grasses, snow, rain, wind, fire or sunshine.

The love of me by nature has placed me in the exact environment where I function well and have an opportunity to grow. Yes, I will hug a tree when I need to feel more grounded. I will lean against them with my back straight and tall to pull their energy into my field. I will continue to be amazed by the forces of my environment.

I have empathy for those who are terrorized, maimed or defiled by the acts of their natural surroundings. I believe we are placed where we are by the contract which was written on the Other Side before reincarnating into this lifetime. Just as my son left this world at age thirty-three, other souls have made similar plans to leave this Earth, albeit too soon by mankind's calculations. By whatever means they have chosen, they too will depart.

"What? You cry! Do you really believe that last paragraph?" Yes, yes, I do. I have studied, I have questioned, and I will pass on the message I received from my channeling today. Of course, I have felt uncertainty pertaining to this theory. As I tell you to question all information you receive, I too have queried others until I turned to my guides for their directives. Each day's direction in my writing is based upon what the Others want me to share with you. And so, I do.

If you get anything from this book, it is to probe into what you read, hear and study all the while loving yourself. Examine, investigate and research until you are satisfied in your entire being.

I am fed all kinds of information and when I doubt or have the slightest instinct that what I am learning may not be so, I write the question down before meditation and thereby responses come, and with it my complete trust of those answers. My Team who leads me with their love and devotion and upon whom I trust without question, have been placed in my life to protect me and love me without judgment. They respond with clear and concise information that I can process with ease and fulfillment.

As this chapter comes to a close, I want to share with you why I included it. As I sit in nature, the solitude becomes a blend of love of me and love of the Earth. This is how I wish to be loved. With a quiet energy exchange with others knowing that all is operating as it should be. Knowing that I have come to this place of love of self at just the right time in my life. I have learned to be more forgiving and less judgmental. I can use discernment to keep me out of energies that do not serve me. I have grown into the person I wish to be for all lifetimes. Since I've learned this, I have been told, I will not have to learn it in the next incarnation should I choose one. I do know that there will be this loving peace that has settled over me as I accept nature's wild rides and smooth sailing. Trusting all in order in the Universe.

Who knows what the Other Side will have in store for me? That one I can't look up. I can see inside the Akashic Records, but that is the past, not the future. So, try as I might, I can't research what is next for my soul when it leaves the Earth. I am not shown how I have chosen to release my soul's energy back into the ethers either.

Do we really choose, on the Other Side, how our release from our worldly body will take place?

It is I, Amadeus, Dear One.

Your question today is a deep one. With what has taken place in your personal life, we know that you are asking once more for the truth. Yet, you are already aware of this fact of vacating your human body.

We feel you are looking for qualification from us. So, we will reassure you that what you are asking will be explained by you in your writings today.

As you sit in council, here on the Other Side, you find out about the lessons you are to learn,

*the reason for your reincarnation and the time
and place of your return to us. You agree to certain things that cannot be changed and some
that will have freewill, by you, in directing them.*

*It is with esteemed pleasure that we find you
seeking the truth from us. It is the reason we are
here, and we delight that you have discovered
us and our happiness for your well-being. You
will teach this to as many who wish to listen and
make changes in their lives. It will also reassure those who believe as you do that we have
answered with complete qualification of your
uncertainty. Ask and we will answer, as always.*

*Go now, continue your book as we lead you
to these profound questions and answers.*

Love, Amadeus.

Meditation and writing are wonderful practices to get into.
They have brought me from the depths of despair to back among
the living. Bringing me "out of the darkness and into the light,"
as it has been said. I love this Earth and appreciate all the acts
of nature that are bestowed upon me, and so Mother Earth
returns that love to me by osmosis.

It is with the blessings of the world we live in that I live and
breathe freely on this planet and give the gift of love to all willing to receive it. This reverence for the energy that is me has
been given to me by those on the Other Side who look out for
my welfare and comfort.

Not all people of the Earth desire the path I have chosen. That does not make them right or wrong. Just as you make the decision, as you read this material, to take it into your heart or reject it, I too had that choice. Imagine my trepidation as I began my journey into this realm of unknowing and uncertainty. As I was lifted from the agony of loss, I was given the gift of spirituality. I could receive it or discard it.

What was the purpose of such heart-wrenching loss if not to assist me in my personal growth? I examined and reexamined all that I was being taught, and it was a conscious decision to receive the information with gratitude for my mental health.

Having made the decision to embrace spirituality, I am more confident that all I am teaching you and others like you is the ultimate truth. I have a passion for what I believe in and seek to guide those who are beginning their search in a positive direction by reinforcing their beliefs and giving them a hand up in their search for the truth as I know it. I ask you, if you differ in opinion, could we please agree to disagree? I know that sounds like a cliché, but I am offering the contents of this book as guidance, not to pressure people into changing their way of thinking.

I will also be there for those who have questions and will answer them with honesty. If they wish to climb on board with me and explore the gifts of the Universe in the same way I have, I will be ready and willing to be their guardian. All I ask in return is that they begin to see the importance of loving the 'me' in me.

CHAPTER XIV

Me, A Writer

Another day has blossomed right before my eyes; a day filled with sunshine and peace in my heart. Roses blooming, birds darting to and fro and a gentle breeze ever so slightly moving the leaves. A new day has dawned with its pages open for me to write on. I am in complete gratitude.

I will fill the morning hours with another chapter. There is so much to know and yet at times I wonder where the fingers will take me as they fly over the keyboard.

Many years ago, as a young high school student, I decided to study typing. I had arranged things in my mind so that, should I need to work in an office, this would be a good subject to drop into my bag of tricks. (Fifty years ago, women became nurses, teachers or secretaries for the most part.)

I proceeded to take all types of office courses. Typing was just the first. After that came shorthand with all its many characters representing letters in the alphabet or phrases that could be grouped together. Bookkeeping and many other office skills found their way onto my schedule each year until my senior year! Then, I could take Office Skills, and, with the instructor's assistance, I was off to find my first job.

The excitement of it all! Hired at the first interview! I would make $1 per hour, working twenty hours per week. I was no longer the neighborhood babysitter at $.50 per hour after school. In a few short weeks after the beginning of the school year, I had doubled my salary and it was consistent. I was on my way to financial freedom! New clothes, and the money to join my sister in purchasing the old family car from my father came soon afterwards. With that, the two-mile trek to my office job and the return home would become so much easier. "Just keep saving that money," I told myself! This mantra has haunted me throughout my life. As much as my husband or I made, I always felt there was never enough. This energy has been tweaked and enough is all I need.

College appeared out of the question. Still, I took the college prep courses that were offered to keep the door open for all possibilities. As the progression of my life continued, there were no funds to further my formal education based on the situation at home. There was no thought of school loans. My family did not live on credit. Everything was paid for in full, except for that set of encyclopedias I referred to earlier and, of course, the house. That's the way it was back then, and I have no adverse emotion tied to that.

Over the years, I have taken many classes at local colleges in Arizona, Washington State, and California; no formal degrees, but that is not what my life is about. It is learning of my choices and following through with them.

You may wonder why I am adding this to my story. In the beginning, I only wanted to type so I could get a job in an office. Yet, here I am, typing my second book. There is amazing synchronicity here. I look for these coincidences every single day and not many days go by without me finding something that could be shuffled off as happenstance, and yet I know it is the wily ways of the Universe teaching me to trust.

It is I, Amadeus. I am here this morning, Sweet One, to enjoy the day with you.

I enjoy all of them, but this one seems special on many levels. The peace you are feeling will come to you more and more as you work through all issues of this life and past lives. They do not scream for attention, but we know what they are and so do you. It is not for the world to know. Some things are private to be known only unto the soul, and to those of us who guide you along your path and protect you from the pitfalls of the world.

Each time you sit with your laptop balanced so steadily on your lap, we visit. One at a time or all at once. We help you choose the subjects and the words for the day. You are moving along swimmingly and with joy in your heart as the chapters unfold in front of you.

Yes, we were there when you learned the keyboard on those big cumbersome typewriters that you pounded on to increase your speed. We were there, too, when your new IBM Selectric showed up on your desk in the classroom. How clumsy you were with the concept of hitting a key for the return instead of that large metal contraption. Your typing tests were blown for weeks as you navigated the keys and gained control of the ease with which you touched the keys and hit the return button.

Then, we were also with you when you touched your first computer. Now, your hands fly across the keyboard and you have assistance with a click of the mouse to correct spelling and punctuation errors.

You chose well, Sweet One. We are applauding the work you did then and the work you do now. Enjoy the story as we write together this day.

Always with love, Amadeus.

I was always meant to be a writer. I have always had excellent writing skills. I remember Kevin's mother telling me how much she enjoyed my letters. She said I left nothing out and felt as though she was visiting us as she read them. Part of what I wrote to her was wordy and filled with anecdotes. Listen to me love the 'me' in me!

Small pieces of that style have been edited out by Jean-Noel (editor of my first book). She taught me that you, the reader, would only want to read the tales that pertain to the story and would mean something to the idea I was trying to express. I send her many blessings of a job well done.

As I sit here in the peace that Amadeus referred to, it is in knowing that my life is changing course. It will be a good change, for with it I will grow and learn more about the world. I have ended my hours of volunteering at the place where I used to teach so that I might concentrate on this volume. I must be ready when the time comes to travel, hold book signings, and teach love of self; loving the 'you' in you.

The teaching of what I know to be true in my heart is what I am looking forward to now. I stayed involved with an institution filled with like-minded people for many years and am happy to take those contacts with me in my heart, my life and on Facebook. Time is now dedicated to me so that I can teach you. Holding classes each week in my current office brings happiness to my soul. Just this week my teaching has exploded into many new classes including my Children's Meditation classes for the summer. How blessed I am to be teaching the children! The amount and titles of the classes will continue to evolve as I do. Also, I have put together a four-part class known as *Trusting What You Already Know,* and it already is forming, and it is time for another Loving the You in You daylong session.

I have witnessed the first inkling in another's mind that Having made the decision to embrace spirituality is their truth, as it is mine. I have watched as they struggled to trust enough to let Spirit take over their pen and let it flow in a new way. Then, I gloried when these same students in my Automatic Writing and Channeling classes spoke their first words from the Other Side. A word not from them, but from their guide. A message for all in the room as they spoke.

For one woman, the first word was "Love". Then, she was quiet as tears began to moisten her cheeks. She was feeling the love vibration from those on the Other Side and those of us in the room. This woman was finished speaking to us for the day but returned each week to bring untold messages of love to the class.

There is a gentleman in class who wishes to write, but not verbalize. He has decided that for him, that is all he needs now. I honor that, and I honor him. He is not allowing anyone to tell him what he needs to be doing. He is choosing as I have asked you to do.

I enjoy each student for the vibration that brings us together. When someone discovers this is not for them, they do not return. I take no negative energy in their decision. I am excited that they have followed their hearts. They may return, or they may move on to other things. I cherish the rights that we must roam free and follow our hearts in the freedom of our country, the United States of America.

This is my book. This is my journey. And so, it is.

CHAPTER XV

The New Me

A s I finished the last chapter and saw how it ended, my thought was that I was through with this book. 'And so, it is' is a phrase often used at the end of a meditation, so it felt like the story was complete.

I questioned friends and family to see the consensus of whether they felt it complete or not. Some felt if it was only thirty-seven pages, then that was fine with them. Then there were others who wanted to hear more from me. They enjoyed getting lost in the first book and wanted more, not less. One psychic friend said, "I feel there is more."

Well, there was not more at that time as I was truly void of thought. I felt I had fallen into an abyss and there was nothing whirling in my mind to move forward. Writer's block, perhaps?

My consultation with my Guides, I should have asked to begin with, brought forth this confirming advice;

> **We are all with you, Dear One.**
>
> **You are questioning the next idea for another chapter. These chapters will continue to unfold just as we have planned and directed thus far. Know that it is with love that we are all working to bring your words to others so that they might understand the complete concept of love of self and how you attained it. You, Sweet One, are the vessel by which the words are written. You are important in this time of the Earth as you have been given the ability to love yourself and to give others the opportunity to feel as you do.**
>   **Go in that vibration and nothing will stop the flow. It is yours to tap into at any time that you wish. We send our love. All of us on the Other Side bring nothing but loving energy to wash your human body and ethereal soul.**
>
> **Sending love to you from Us.**

Knowing there was more to come, my writing flow interrupted, I was off to other tasks that needed to be taken care of not realizing that the errand at hand would be part of the story. Synchronicity at its finest.

That afternoon I decided to return a wallet I had purchased at a local chain store. When I purchased it, it was the least expensive one on the shelf. Alas, when I got home and went to transfer the old cards to the new one, I didn't like the organization of the wallet.

As I walked back into the store and perused the shelf, I found the perfect item and it was half the price! Oh, thank you for leading me there on that day, Guides and Others.

Cruising through the store, my savings of twelve dollars quickly was lost on the clothes and toys for my grandson's first birthday the following day! There were at least forty outfits to buy, but I settled on two.

Standing in line, awaiting the next cashier to ring up my purchases, a man walked to the front of the line oblivious of the six people he had walked in front of. They stood there staring at his back with aggravation written all over their faces, but he was not moved by their energy. I said to him, "Excuse me, sir, but the end of the line is back there." He boldly looked at me and said, "I was in line, but wanted another item." Then, the tirade began!

"You should keep your nose out of other people's business. It would serve you to keep your eyes to yourself and your mouth shut," he said. These may not be the exact words that were spoken, but you get the idea of the energy with him at that moment.

I quietly voiced, "Thank you for the advice. I will consider it. Have a blessed day."

The others in line looked at me with wide eyes and shook their heads. I'm sure they wondered why I was so passive, considering his behavior. Inside I knew I was at peace. I didn't have time to react any differently nor would I have wanted to. He was tall, big and obviously in a not-so-happy space that day. I was strong and not intimidated yet remained polite and gentle.

I was in the Light and stayed centered while remaining true to the new me.

Who was this man who vanished as I made my way to pay for my purchases? I believe it was a Guide showing me how I had changed. Yes, my face turned red, public eyes upon me, awaiting my reaction. But, the old unloved me was no longer there.

There was no reason to sit back and take these words without acknowledging him. He wanted to be heard. He needed to speak, albeit with wrath and disdain. By gently loving me and putting forth positive reactions to a difficult moment, the scene was diffused. Any other reaction would have escalated the situation.

I have had energy from the Other Side show up in other ways that were more loving. In the months after my father's passing many years ago, I found myself in the local grocery store. As I took my change, I noticed an elderly gentleman reminiscent of my father standing beside me. He began to softly sing the words; "you are the wind beneath my wings." ("Wind Beneath My Wings" is a song written in 1982 by Jeff Silbar and Larry Henley. It was sung by Bette Midler in the 1989 movie *Beaches*.) Tears stung my eyes as I had played that song for my father while in his hospital bed and had asked if we could play it at his funeral. He was so pleased, that he teared up and nodded his approval. I knew my father had come to visit me that day through this man.

As I grew into adulthood, the turmoil of childhood was mended somewhat. Not to be forgotten, but to be ignored and my parents became closer to my heart. I still did not feel love from them and they never said they loved me, but they showed respect.

There have been other instances of signs from the souls who have crossed over, too many to share here, but I enjoy the following one. I know every time I find a single penny that my son has popped in to say hello. They show up in the most unusual places. When we moved into our latest home, the movers unrolled the family room carpet and there, right in the middle of the carpet, was a shiny penny, heads up. The penny was to remind me that he was here and approved of our space. While looking for a home this time, he asked me to walk in the gardens. I didn't know what that meant until one day I noticed the name of our neighborhood carried the word 'Gardens'. It was at that moment I smiled and realized he had chosen this home.

Since the days that I began to pay attention, there have been numerous signs that those on the Other Side are truly with me. Listen without judgment and you will hear messages also. Follow their guidance.

My favorite story, included in my first book, is about hearing and not listening. As I put the open glass of milk in the refrigerator in my home in Bellevue, WA many years ago, I heard a thought. The thought came through as a voice in my head, "Don't put that in there without a lid. It will spill, and you will be angry that you have to clean it up!" Of course, busy mommy knows she will remember, and she will be careful when she opens the fridge next time so ignores that routine message.

Seriously? The busy multi-tasking mommy is going to retain such mundane information? I scurried around cleaning, doing laundry, playing with the children and then it was time for lunch. How many hundreds of thoughts had run through my mind that morning? I pulled open the door of the fridge; lo and behold, the milk spilled!

Yes, there I was putting myself down with negative thoughts and demeaning myself for not listening to 'the voice I had heard' earlier. At that time, I did not know it was a message from the Other Side. There I was, in the middle of another busy day, taking time, I really didn't feel I had, to clean the entire refrigerator as the milk was not on the bottom shelf, but on the top, and the liquid had found its way into every crease and crevice. I know now those who had whispered to me to put a lid on the small plastic cup were watching with sadness while I crouched on my knees cleaning up the milk, and literally crying over it!

I implore you, listen and trust. Trust, trust, trust. This is what I wish for you in this lifetime. I wish you to love the 'you' in you so much that you learn to listen to these wonderful energies that exist for you and that you find things around you moving with ease and light. The more you build on the love of self and the trust that there are Others on the Other Side, the easier things can fall into place. Manifest the best there is by following this advice.

Another chapter has unfolded.

It is I, Amadeus, greeting you this day, Beloved.

Yes, there is more to the story you are sharing. You have had, and will continue to have, synchronicities and enlightenments. And, yes, the man in the store was placed in your energy field to show you your growth and conviction.

This was a 'test' so to speak. It was to show you how you have changed and how, in difficult circumstances, you can react out of love and not out of disdain. You had not walked in that man's shoes on that day. He wanted to make a

purchase and not be spoken to. You will be finding more similar men and women as you take to the road and raise your voice to the masses. Not all will love and adore you. Yet, you will respond in a loving manner. It does set them thinking. It does help them realize they may have been out of place with their words or actions. Don't expect to change them as they are on their own journey but respect their passage and answer their comments with loving words.

Spirituality has been brought to your voyage in this incarnation. This lifetime is not like others where you hid in dark corners to speak as you speak here, now. This is a life where you can write a book like this on and speak whatever you wish so that your messages are heard.

Agree to disagree has been used in conversation with you and others many times. Continue the notion and make it a part of the bag of tools you carry in your mind and heart.

No one is correct one hundred percent of the time, so expect confrontation and expect to be questioned as you were in your exchange with the unhappy man on Saturday.

Remember Dear One, we are all with you always and love you deeply, Amadeus.

CHAPTER XVI

Learning How to Heal the Earth

My class on Tuesday night extended later than usual. There were just three of us that evening, but the chemistry flowed between us and conversations of synchronicity filled the hours before nine o'clock. We had not even begun to channel when I announced the time. We decided, together, to stay for another half hour so we could hear the messages that were yet to flow through our minds and voices.

Amadeus was first, as usual. He began and welcomed all in the room and acknowledged the need for self-love. Tonight, there was more to his message of healing the earth through love. It made perfect sense that he did this now as I had been questioning how we were going to accomplish this mighty feat. He had said it would not be in this lifetime of mine, but that I would witness this in another place and time.

Then we heard,

> **"You are leading them through what they have come to hear, Dear One. Know that the love vibration you are teaching will flow beyond this world. It will remain deeply embedded in all souls who learn to love themselves. When they depart this world and ultimately reincarnate, they will bring this vibration with them. It will not be forgotten as it has been for eons.**
>
> **Thusly, when they return and bring this joy and peace with them, they will be born to parents who have learned love of self and will know how to keep its energy flowing. This will continue for many generations, but it begins with you. It begins with the three of you. (The three of us in class that night.) It will extend in your families and your community. Know you are the hope that heals the planet.**
>
> **Go in love, Amadeus."**

Wow! That is what I'd been missing! I hadn't been able to see how, as we cycle in and out of the Earth's energy that we could keep the momentum going to achieve the healing of the planet. I had been taught that I was to lead those who heard my message. I trusted Amadeus completely. If I were to take this concept public, I would need to know how to explain the phenomenon I was proposing. This was part of the puzzle I had been trying to piece together ever since the messages of self-love were brought to me. This was an amazing introspection as to how the treatment to the soul would take place.

I move forward knowing that many on the Earth now are experiencing the same message as the internet and the book stores gradually fill with books about love of one's self. There are many twists and turns and methods, but all point towards the same goal, and we shall attain it simultaneously.

The other messages touched on self-love and peace through-out the world, where starvation and fear would no longer exist. Where human beings would behave with loving acts of kindness and blessed emotions would resonate deep within the souls of all. When you are living in a love vibration, you cannot fathom destructive power, obliteration of lives and starvation.

The ladies and I launched into a deep conversation filled with serious chatter and bursts of laughter. We so enjoyed ourselves that 9:45 p.m. caught us by surprise. We gathered our journals and purses together, embraced and headed out into the night. So much to think about on the drive home.

Thursday morning, February 5, 2015, my morning class met and six of us introduced ourselves and revealed the synchro-nicities which had dotted our week. We caught up and chatted about our thoughts and questions. I shared the message from Tuesday evening and we dove into conversation! It was the opening of a very auspicious class.

One of the amazing women in class had a story about two small clear glass angels she had on her mantel. Her mother's spirit came to visit the evening before class and revealed that this spirit's sister was passing in the nursing home where she resided. At that very moment, one of the glass angels crashed to the floor and broke into infinite pieces. As this dear woman was cleaning the floor of the glass debris, the telephone rang. Yes, you guessed, I'm sure, that the aunt in the nursing home had crossed into the light that very evening.

While we are aware of the truth in synchronicity and spirit messages, the uncanny part of this morning class was the message I received the evening before; ***"There will be a friend on your journey tomorrow who will need to be heard. There is a crossing expected in her family and although she is not extremely close to the soul who is leaving, she will want to sit with a group of like-minded people who will assist her in processing the grief that has only just begun. This grieving woman is in the beginning stages of learning to love herself and you will hold her up and support her in this next step of her journey. It is why she has been placed by us, here on the Other Side, into your current group of loving, supportive women. Continue to teach and she, too, will help heal the Earth."***

It became increasingly clear that the missive of Amadeus was to be shared with all who would listen. This message was going to become the second most important piece of information in this book. The first, of course, was the concept that you can learn to love the 'you' in you! Now, we had the explanation as to how this newfound love we are learning and teaching about was going to help realize our heart's desire; healing the Earth.

I am enthusiastic about bringing this information to you through this book and equally excited to have Amadeus continue to bring it forward during my monthly talks at public venues throughout Southern California and Arizona.

During a lunch with my dear friend, Sherri, we chatted about this new breakthrough and have planned an evening with Amadeus. She, the ever provider of nourishment, having owned her own restaurant at one-time, suggested tea and crackers. I, having learned that Amadeus' favorite city was Vienna, made the decision to have Vienna Fingers. It is a delicately sweet cookie that I enjoyed as a child but had never purchased as an adult. Sherri thought that was a grand idea as her sweet-tooth always finds itself rearing its head during our meals together.

That evening will be planned and promoted so that all those in attendance will hear Amadeus' words with their own ears and therefore be better able to understand how this healing is going to work. I am thrilled beyond belief that Amadeus has chosen me to bring this message to the world in whatever way he deems possible.

In early December of last year, I asked when I was going to be bringing this message out to the public and was told that 'they' needed six months to put the pieces in place. I have begun the six months with writing this book and slowing my volunteering time.

When a call comes to talk of this concept of self-love and healing Gaia, I will be off to do what I was born to do, and fulfill my agreements conjured up on the Other Side in counsel. Yes, I am ready.

(As I edit this chapter, I am pleased to announce that our plan with Sherri came to be, with an event held at Spirit's Child in Tucson, Arizona. "Coffee, Tea, Amadeus and Me" was presented on August 20, 2016. I was excited beyond words to take this event to my home town and visit friends and family, all the while making new friends who will share their energy with me!

It was also revisited the weekend of November 2016, June 2017 and November 2017. The event has gained in popularity and continues to bring recovery of their pain to many.)

It is I, Amadeus. Good morning, Dear One!

As you write this morning, I feel your excitement in knowing how to explain to the world how this healing will work. You have an amazing gift of conversation. With it you will accomplish what we have asked of you. Yes, you did agree to do this before you incarnated.

I am deeply moved and proud to be able to assist you in your purpose here this lifetime. It is so beautiful to see the soul you have always been. Forgiving me for our lifetime together of little brother and big sister has cleansed the soul energy of who I was then, Wolfgang Amadeus Mozart. Through the lessons here on the Other Side, I have been able to see the error of my ways in other lifetimes.

As we return to the Earth with new lessons to learn, we bring with us the energy of the lessons we have already learned. I have chosen not to reincarnate, but to remain here to assist you and clear the Karma of that lifetime so many years ago.

It cleanses my energy to do this. This is not a selfish act on my part, but a selfless one. It brings such joy and pleasure to all in your soul group. We have traveled with this group for many lifetimes. Everyone you have traveled with, whether on the Earth now, or on the Other Side, is cheering you on! They are applauding you and your actions.

Your gentle soul keeps many in check. They stop in their drama when you do not join them. When you cry out for assistance, know that many, both there and here, are jumping through hoops to assist. You are the very essence of love and support.

We recognize you are up for the challenge and assure you it will be just that. At times, you will grow weary. But, know that we are all here to hold you up as you go the extra mile for humanity.

Yes, the message was a long one this day, but has been needed. You need to be able to express love, appreciation and thanks at this time as you propel yourself forward on this important step of your journey.

Go in love, light and laughter, Amadeus!

CHAPTER XVII

Meeting Archangel Gabriel

O n a recent Tuesday evening during a guided meditation in my *Writing with my Dream Muse* class led by Marjorie Miles, I experienced a new sensation on the top of my head, on the right side. This was a phenomenon that had never occurred before. It was the same tingling feeling I get when others from beyond visit, but in a new location.

"Who is with me?" I ask.

"Gabriel," I hear."

"Archangel Gabriel?" I query.

"Yes, I have come to build upon the theory of love of self. Tonight, you will introduce it to your group as a most prestigious rite of passage. They will help to spread the word to those they know and your message for them will move through their circles and continue to raise the concept of love of self. It will, one day, shift the energy of the Earth."

We are always given a few minutes to write after meditation, delivering whatever message or story that was generated during this quiet time. I am usually a very quick writer. This evening, however, there is a deliberate slowness of my penmanship. It is large and straight up and down. It's nothing at all like the small curvy letters that usually flow from my pen. I found myself needing an extra minute to get the last few words of his dictation out of my head and onto the journal page.

Most times, I am one of the first to lay down my pen and wait for the others to finish their writing. That night, I wrote long after Marjorie said the time was up. She reminds us we can continue these writings later, but this would not wait. This was an important message being passed to me and was not something I could conjure up in the days to come. Immediately, I was to share this message with this group

I am amazed! I have many who come to me from the Other Side, but it is the first time I have written with Archangel Gabriel and he was delivering a message, personally, to the class of seven. They have all heard me talk of self-love and of this book. Yet, this is the first time they have witnessed the channeling and automatic writing I so lovingly describe to them. Many have read my first book and know my history.

This was a magical evening where I could deliver the message of love of self to these men and women and see the impact it made on them by the expressions on their faces. Since we are all spiritual, they get it. They understand the concept completely, even though many do not channel or even wish to.

There are many modalities in aving made the decision to embrace spirituality and, while we practice these senses, some prefer to stay where they are and just enjoy the beauty of knowing and loving. There is not always a need to move forward in something new. After all, there is conscious choice.

As I have said before, I have studied healing modalities that do not resonate with me. I experienced them but did not hold onto them. I am a natural healer and do not need symbols and rituals to heal others. I use my own energy and send it out so that another's energy might receive it and be healed.

I have enjoyed automatic writing and channeling since I first discovered them and am pleased with that. I have made a connection with my Guides and Angels who assist me whenever I ask them to. I can go through life ignoring their presence or I can rely on them to bring me sage advice for whatever is in my path that I need assistance with. Receiving the love given so freely by those who reside on the other side of the veil intrigues me. After many lifetimes of not feeling loved enough (whatever that means to me) I have found a way to fill my heart, head, belly and soul with that which I so desired on every level of my being.

The messages brought to me from the Other Side are always loving and caring. Even when I am being taught some element that I need for my soul to grow, I am shown through loving expressions. It is easy to move into a place of self-love when you are being treated with such kindness and compassion.

I have been taught by my Team not to be envious and to focus on self-love. I have been guided to learn that anger does not serve me. The gentleness that is used for my self-improvement has taught me to be kinder and gentler with myself and others. Patience has become a part of my essence through their teachings. I embrace the teachings that come through my writing and channeling. They are helping to evolve me into a more lovable human who asks for their guidance.

Good Morning Beautiful One!

This is Archangel Gabriel speaking with you this day. It was such a pleasure to finally talk with and through you that Thursday evening not so long ago.

I have come to sit with you as you continue to work with us on the notion that everyone will learn to love themselves on a deep soul level during the next generations. Once this has been mastered, you will always reincarnate with the experience woven deep into the crevices of your soul energy.

We cannot explain why there are so many of you who do not understand this concept. It has been lost through the centuries of man believing he must be King and rule the land instead of sharing the bounty with all who are present. It is truly life changing, yet we believe ego can and will be changed for the betterment of mankind.

We wish for you to always retain this infor-mation now and forevermore. It has changed you, and it will change all others who have not felt this undying love for themselves.

It may seem uncanny that I have chosen to show up now in this time and space and, yet it is exactly when and where you selected to have my identity made known. You do not realize that you asked for this to happen when it did.

You do not often sit in 'guided' meditation awaiting a message from us. This was the first opportunity for you to slow your mind and relax among like-minded friends who love you with-out question. They must strongly believe in what we are asking of them as they all touch the lives of the little ones we need to reach. I will leave you now knowing I will return each time you ask for me and sometimes when you haven't. You know how we vie for your willingness to bring us through.

Sitting in love of you, Archangel Gabriel.

It is I, Amadeus, Dear One, also greeting you this day.

You asked to be placed in this warm part of the country even though you did not realize it at the time. Here you can sit in the warmth of the day and listen to the birds as they sing their songs, communicating their messages to each other.

Spring seems to have already found its way into Southern California. Be aware, though, that there can always be a setback. Keep your warm clothes clean and ready. Do not put them away for the summer just yet.

Simply beautiful was the message from Archangel Gabriel. He was certainly a surprise to you and yet we all knew he was with you, awaiting a time to present himself. We, on the Other Side, surround you.

There are many on the earth plane who teach this concept of self-love. We wish for you to be out there also, representing mankind as a wife, mother, grandmother, sibling and friend.

You have all the qualities we are looking for and when we planned this, long before you reincarnated, we all knew you would find the time later in life when you could sit with us and follow your dreams.

Your loving energy that attracts those from all walks of life emanates from your energy field with ease and grace. Many recognize this quality as soon as they step into it. Some are taken aback and feel small. These are some of the ones we wish to have you teach. You know that you are not more special than they and you enjoy seeing them rise in their gifts radiating in the love they have discovered.

Continue to teach; in person, on the tele-phone, social media, tele-seminars and through your books. You, Dear One, are truly appreciated on Earth and here, on the Other Side.

Go in love and light this day, Amadeus.

As a postscript to this session, it is now March 2, 2015. On Saturday, winter returned to Southern California just like I had been advised. It began to rain that evening and continued through the weekend. Today, it hailed on the beach and snowed in the mountains. Ski season has returned with a vengeance and my warm clothes were ready. Thanks, guys, for guiding me in the right direction this week.

As I have related to you before, I am teaching classes on Automatic Writing/Channeling. The concept of this type of writing was explained in a previous chapter.

The daytime class, surprisingly, has a steady flow of students. Some drive an hour to sit in meditation, to be counseled in faith and trust, and to hear from those on the Other Side. The night class draws fewer students, yet they all come for the same reason the daytime students appear. There are few day classes offered in our community and there are many who seek the answers to their questions, and so it is that these are filled. I am blessed with sufficient free time to provide these additional day classes for the seekers.

Who do I think I am that I can be a teacher? What makes me feel competent enough to share what I have learned with those who have not met me before? It comes with love of self and a passion to share what I have learned on this journey so far. In class, I teach what I know to be my truth. Many of my students have been on their journey for some time and they, occasionally, also have things to teach me. I listen, absorb and then investigate on my own time. Whenever I am learning something new, I continue to delve into the information at my fingertips for absolute resonance. I know my Team leads me through each class.

As you are aware, I did not step easily onto this path of Spirituality. I came for solace, for answers to questions I had asked of myself in this life time. Who are we, really? What are we doing here? What is the purpose of me being here now? What happens after the soul leaves the body? Why did my son move on before me?

If you have ever had a reason to ask any of these questions, in any form, I have come to explain what I have learned about seeking the answers. Just as I teach those who enter my classroom, I will share what I know and leave you with more questions.

In last night's class, we began with the usual guided meditation. One of the women I have known for a few years now, had totem signs appear in her meditation; a hummingbird, a butterfly and a grasshopper. As we looked them up in my trusty little book, "Pocket Guide to Spirit Animals: Understanding the Messages from Your Animal Spirit Guides" by Steven Farmer, they all led in the same direction. "Change is coming, trust that it is near and have patience," was the repeated message.

She is ready to accept the change but is having some trouble being patient and trusting that the Universe is setting up this shift. She wonders why it is taking so long. As we chatted, I reminded her that she was the one who had written this agreement before she returned to the Earth for the lessons she needed to learn during this current incarnation. She laughed as we both agreed; we wish we would have read the small print!

Her husband left the Earth at about the same time she became a student in my class. I befriended her as she took her first tentative steps back into a practice she had let go of, spirituality. It is often at this vulnerable time that many come searching for answers to their questions. There are several schools and facilities where people seeking answers can learn to communicate with those who have passed from the energy of this earth plane.

I will begin with the 'who are we?' synopsis. We are energy. First and foremost. We have come into the world many times and lived many lives. Some lives have been recreated on other planets where we exist in different forms. Having visited some of my past lives in meditation or regression, I have seen myself always as a healer of souls. In the past, I have also been a teacher.

Healing and teaching walk hand in hand. When you work as a healer, you teach those you are helping to mend an issue and how to continue recovering on their own. These two modalities come in myriad ways through me. Energy therapies, counseling, psychic and mediumship readings, and Hypnotherapy, just to name a few.

As I counsel souls and help them in seeing the bigger picture, I am teaching them ways to stay in the energy of all that they are learning. It is extremely easy to slip back into our old habits and once again become distraught at our losses. When I catch myself being my old self, and not loving the me in me, I stop what I'm doing and gently ground myself in that vibration of love.

When someone I am counseling falls back into their 'poor me' place, I quietly utter a few words which are instrumental in bringing them back into focus. These words are different for everyone. Each of us is working on our own issues and we, at times, need the loving support of someone else who can see our slide backward. We may not even see our own, but we can see when others are struggling. It is often easier to look at another's life and to help them than it is to look at one's own.

Never belittle yourself for not seeing your own obstacles. Seeing the road blocks in someone else's life is far easier than knowing your own soul. When you catch yourself being less than patient with your own shortcomings, acknowledge the action and seek to change the trigger that pulled the emotion into focus.

Moving to the time when the soul leaves the body, we transition into the light where we are greeted by those who left before us. There is untold love that surrounds the soul group you travel in. On the other side of the veil, you continue to work on the struggles you did not conquer while you were here. You shift the energy of your soul into a place filled with light and not darkness.

It is difficult for me to acknowledge that some departing souls are not ready to go to the light for whatever reason known only unto them. Their energy can sometimes become locked in the vacuum of the Earth as they struggle with unresolved issues. I have yet to encounter one of these energies and feel blessed by that, but I know of others who have struggled. I am becoming more secure in my ability to heal and yet, am not sure I could heal one who is not ready to leave the environment here. It is their story, after all. We have each mapped our own path and there can be no judgment as to what is right or wrong for any other living human.

As I revisit this chapter, rewriting and editing, I am in the process of helping someone cross into the Light. He has been here since the late 1900's and has begun to make his spirit known to a friend of mine. My buddy has called on me to help him with the energy who has come forward in his workplace at night. I have meditated and asked my Team to tell me what they know about this male energy, and how I might assist.

This is what I wrote before meditation on March 17, 2017; "There is a young boy in the grade school here in Orange, CA. What can you tell me, and how can we send him to the light?"

This is their reply:

"Greetings Dear One.

We are here to tell you about Tommy. He comes from many centuries ago.

He and his family were brutally killed in a fire that raged across the valley where the school now sits. He lost contact with them and died alone. He is stuck as he is afraid to move forward alone. The soul of your friend is someone he recognizes from that lifetime. He feels safe now. Safe to show himself. Should you wish to send him to the Light, know that he is ready.

The dream your friend told you about was not a dream at all. It was night flying and this man is being invited to take this boy to the Light. The child's family awaits him.

You are to tell your friend to pray and evoke Tommy's spirit to reach for his mother's hand.

He is to assure Tommy that he is a friend and ready to help him.

On the Other Side, he will be reunited with his family and they will bless your Dear Friend for his caring commitment to send Tommy to them. There is no fear My Love. Have this friend sit, eyes closed, and see Tommy's mother in a long dress. Her hair is pulled up in a bun. He will see Tommy and his mother reunite. He will see them moving away, hand in hand. All will be at peace.

Love to you and your friend from us, Tommy's Angels."

It is I, Amadeus, Dear One. Good morning to you this day.

Yes, it is easy to see you as a healer and a teacher. They do walk hand in hand and as you rise each day in gratitude to be a part of this Universe you greet another opportunity to love and heal others. You have come so very far on your journey in this lifetime and in other lifetimes. With each reincarnation, you rise further forward to becoming love itself. You give love so freely and are easily hurt by the actions of others. It is this character trait we are going to be working on in the coming months. We will protect you as often as we can, but for you to grow in this sector, there must be times when the injustice comes, and you work through it with us.

Your audience loves you and yet, some are not evolved enough to avoid envying your new station in life. They will want what you have and will undoubtedly try to get close to you for the excitement of your journey.

Know that those who truly love you will be there to stand with you unabashedly. Those who are there just for the thrill, will fall away in a moment's notice as something more exciting grabs their attention.

We are here to help you discern the love of you. We are here to keep you safe and satisfied with the good that you are doing in the world, and the attention you will be getting just for being you. Go now, rise from the chair and seize the day filled with wonder and life.

Much love to you, Amadeus.

CHAPTER XVIII

Continuing My Story

As I spoke to my students in class on Thursday morning, Archangel Gabriel's energy came through. He is still new to me, and I am enjoying his banter and his teachings. His message is also about loving one's self, although he verbalizes it a bit differently than Amadeus. He talked about how the child loses his self-love as he grows in society. It seems the perfect time to address some of these issues.

Sports are very competitive, and a vulnerable youngster can be crushed by the taunts of others. Report cards can also set the tone for a child's self-love and self-respect. These are just two examples of man-made issues that attack children's love of self. Is it really that they wish to be so perfect, or is this something being learned from society and its formation of what we all should be? After all, each child is born in perfection and these rules serve to numb that memory.

Parents are proud of the child who brings home stellar grades and then runs up and down the soccer field scoring the winning kick! I don't wish to criticize parents or tell them how to raise productive children. I wish only to address one of the concerns I have recognized as part of the pattern where the little babes begin to question whether they are good enough.

Do you remember a time when you wished only to please your parents? It may have been for a gesture of love or they may have created a reward system for you to reach your highest potential, as they saw it. The key here, is 'as they saw it'. You, as a child, may not have even considered playing a sport or participating in a spelling bee. Yet, there you were in so many outside activities that you didn't have time to relate to the family. You just had to keep succeeding.

Parents, in most households, hope for a better life for their children than the one they had. Why is this? Are they trying to live vicariously through their offspring? Often, they are. It is a typical reaction as the human mind sets out to make all things better than before. Are they better? Or are they just different? Usually, children are not invited to map out the course of their own lives as they are still small and unworldly. How could they possibly have any input into things they know nothing about? Yes, they wrote the big picture on the Other Side before they were born, but some of it must be orchestrated by their parents until they are old enough to begin making decisions of their own.

As a parent, myself, I have known the joy of having my children receive honors in school and in sports. I beamed as they rose to walk to the front of the stage (whatever that stage might have been) to receive their trophy or certificate. It meant to me, at the time, that I was doing a stellar job in the eyes of the leaders and the parent peers. Unaware that it was actually love for me I was seeking at those times, I was disappointed, too, when they were not recognized. I told myself the regret was for their embarrassment, but was it? Or, was it really mine? Ponder this thought for more than a minute and see if you have ever fit into this circumstance.

This is not about critiquing you or me. It is about society and what it has done with the remembrance that they/we did their/our best. We judge us, and we judge them, and, in reality, what does that do to make the world a better place? We must all quit judging ourselves and others. If we stay committed to our individual journey and bring about our own enlightenment, we will be able to share that concept and that energy with all those with whom we come into contact.

Realizing it might be you, as a parent, making decisions that do not even interest your children, are you ready to examine the true reasons you are pushing them? First, you will have to answer the question presented with utmost honesty. Are you aiming to right a wrong that was done to you by your own parents or sibling, peer or teacher, when you were a child? To prove to them some notion, something they were not even aware of, that molded the 'you' that you are today? Not allowing you to participate in a certain sport or not having the money to help you pursue your desires are two common criticisms of children for their parents. Contemplate this question before you begin to formulate a retort. I implore that you explore this idea without judgment of you or your perfection. Your ability to do the best you can with what you know at any given time is all you can claim for yourself.

Understand this is not a condemnation of any part of you. You are perfect, remember? As flawless as we are, there are things in this world that affect us and change our perspectives. Sometimes, we need to silence our 'stories' and glean the truth about what we know now in comparison to what we knew as little ones who were being guided by our parents the best way they knew how at the time.

I am not a therapist. I am merely posing a series of questions for you to bring to the forefront and consider them. As parents, we frequently find the need to reexamine our feelings, versus the reality of our youth. What were the underlying factors which created the adults we are today? I have told my story as I saw it unfold in my youth. Reassessment, as I wrote this story of my childhood, has brought me clarity and a new perspective of how my parents perceived my childhood, and how I may have been a much different, more permissive influence while parenting the four energies who chose me to be their mother.

My children chose me the same way I chose who was to bring me forth into the world and mold the very essence of that energy in this current lifetime. I would love to think of myself as the absolute epitome of the perfect director of my children's lives yet know that that is not the reality. Being brought up in chaos, I worked as hard as I could to create an upbeat, and more loving home life. I excelled on some days and failed on others, but still feel that I failed less often as I grew older. Alas, I am human and know there are many things that could have been altered. Yes, I am pleased that my children are functioning in society at the level that is perfect for them.

A year ago, I might have claimed a hard-won victory for the perfection of my children; the fruit of my body. I might even have been so bold as to state that I was a better parent than those who parented me. Today, with love of self and all that is of my realm, I know that I am simply doing the best I can, which is also what my mom and dad did. Unfortunately, I didn't allow them that credit when they were here in human form. It has taken a lifetime of experience and my spiritual base to understand what took place all those many years ago.

I came prepared today to write this book using the guidance gifted me from the Other Side and from the familiar lessons this life has shown me.

Those on the Other Side include my parents, my son, a brother and sister, and all the other energies from my soul group who have passed before me. My Guides, Angels and Elementals, my Team are helping me become a more loving, dedicated spirit.

It's quite difficult to write about what is right or wrong when raising a child. I know there is a deep well of information for me to dig into. Therefore, I will also read and research the ideas I am presenting here. I invite you to do the same. These are just the tidbits of knowledge I have learned that will whet both your appetite and mine to push us to the point where we are not looking for more.

In the future, as I am presented with more evidence about this journey I am on, whether positive or negative, and more data is revealed, there will be yet another presentation from me. It may be in the form of a book or it may be in the public forum where I am questioned about what I know and am invited to discover and discuss any new developments that are evading me here and now.

It is I, Amadeus, Sweet One.

I am here with you this morning to congratulate you for continuing to press forward with this publication. It will soon be complete and in the hands of the editor and publisher. You are the vessel who is going to be questioned regarding the contents of this manuscript. I want to remind you that you are never alone. We are always with you and will stand and speak as needed. You are never to fear that you are exploiting a notion you cannot support.

There are others in this realm and on the earth plane who will support all your data. The answer that will come into your psyche will, when needed, be our words. This is not to say you are lacking in the knowledge to provide intelligent answers to the questions that will be hurled at you. It is only a gentle reminder that we are always with you. It is the energy of us here on the Other Side who have prodded you to write this text.

You knew about all the evidence you speak of. You had just not fathomed that it would be asked of you to become the conduit in order to bring this to fruition. You are not alone in this endeavor here on the Earth.

There are others who are also in agreement with your ideas and convictions. We are pressing you here, to find out who these individuals are and to laud them. Be in contact with them. Share ideas and bring forth the magic of your message to the Universe.

This is not to be savored in your hometown, but throughout the world. When you were lacking in loving you, the idea of presenting anything to the public alarmed you. Now that you have conquered that emotion, you will be able to address with sweet knowledge that all you say is the truth of all that is. I leave your writing now but am always with you.

Love, Amadeus.

CHAPTER XIX

Learning to Live
with Discernment

I have become friends with some of the young people who have been visiting, teaching and taking classes in the facility where I teach. We have grown to love the energy of each other. In my life, before awakening to spirituality, I would not have thought to befriend them. I was, at that time, a middle-aged woman who critically judged young people who did not fit into the tight mold I had created for those who could enter my exclusive inner circle. After discovering spirituality, I found it necessary to crack open this cold, mean side of me and open myself to the love of others who did not necessarily fit into my box. I am thrilled to say that, because of this new outlook towards others and getting to know them for who they are rather than for the package they are tied up in, I have formed many new relationships that serve to feed my soul. Hence, my box collapsed, and a paper bag was created to rid myself of my rigid and outdated opinions. One day, I will toss the bag and be over that energy completely. Excited to say I've even run a yellow light as I test the sides of that bag.

Bringing back into focus the people who judged others by their oddities, me and my then friends, does the above description sound like someone we would have reason to befriend? To most of you, these young people I have been meeting sound like amazing humans. Yet, according to my own code, however misconceived, there would have been many reasons to never resonate with them.

Some had blue, lavender or pink hair, or any of the rainbow-colored strands in otherwise black, brown or blond hair! There were those with tattoos, and those who embraced crystals as though they were loving friends. Rings and studs found a place for them in their noses and lips. As I observed these young people and felt their energy, I backed away. They didn't fit into my box of what was right and wrong. That was the theory I would have applied to them in years gone by. Oh, my goodness, I have since learned not to judge. I remain in awe.

As I came to know the adolescents in my new circle and saw the excitement in their eyes as they discussed what they knew about spirituality, I found them to be bright, alive and filled with wonder at everything they had learned, and the direction their lives were taking them. They are positive and loving. With an entirely new perspective, I began to embrace their energy and was filled with the warm love of who they were.

I have gotten used to the people who are different than those tucked away in my old box. Most of the people in my days prior to my spiritual enlightenment do not share the enjoyment I find within the embrace of spirituality. In fact, there is only Lynn, the woman with whom I began this part of my journey and who also attends the Holistic Faires at the facility where I played for so long and at the new places where I give readings or have organized an event. The women at the old job have continued on their journeys, but most no longer are in contact. My dear friend Lisa who introduced me to her sister Lori, the psychic I spoke of many chapters ago, is still close and we meet every few months for an hour or five to fill our heads and hearts with each other's accomplishments and let downs. She and I have loved each other unconditionally for over fifteen years now.

The remainder of old friends are perusing other passions. I choose not to judge them either. They are exactly in the place their contract designated them to be. Yes, we have free will, but some choose not to use it. Perhaps those souls will wait until another lifetime to discover what I have found in this one. Perhaps they will never seek out spirituality at all. I wish them only to find love of self whenever they are ready and keep it close to their heart, teaching it to their children and grandchildren.

The reason I have touched on the subject of these young souls in this chapter is because of a Blog that Rebecca Nguyen had on her website. As a side note, she had pink hair when we met. I felt it would be interesting to query her Guide about love of self. I was exhilarated that the author was open to inviting others to ask questions of her Guide. I did not ask questions because I needed some validation of what I was being taught by my own friends on the Other Side, but because I wanted you to hear the message about self-love as shared by someone else's Guide.

Here is my question:

"Could you please bring forth your views on self-love ultimately being able to heal the Earth of the wars, famine and strife? Thank you and Blessed Be."

Hello and Namaste!

Self-love is the topic of the day. It is our true essence of self that we forget when we grow old. We are what we choose to become, so we can be the bread or the mold.

We don't grow old if we choose to believe we are young at heart, and when we are young at heart we connect with our inner child, which is our pure essence of love. By choosing to self-love, you are giving yourself the best gift ever (and its free!). It literally costs nothing to love yourself, to wake up in the morning and say, "I AM AWESOME!" But not many of you do this, and that is why I speak to you today. I want to remind you of your essence. You might know other words for it, like your soul or your connection with All-That-Is. Your essence is the same as your neighbor's, your cat's essence, the essence of that fancy hedge with the trimmings, the essence of that mysterious stain on your carpet that won't wash out, the essence of your perceived worst enemy. Essence simply is everything that is.

So how is this self-love supposed to end famine, war, and strife? It is fact that we call this energy love, and this is what connects us all. Remember the circle of life? It speaks of the spirit also as what "moves us all." For what we are is what moves us, and we are moved by what we are through other people, the situations we find ourselves in, the feelings we have for one another, and the thoughts that they bring about. We are all connected. She is, he is, you are me. They are all you, and once you understand this, you are one step closer to accepting life. It starts with the realization that you are love. You, without the context of the external world. You detached from said world. You, recognizing your soul's perfection. You, knowing that your thoughts and actions are intentions to co-create with the Universe.

You, you, you. It all starts with you. You, taking more time to self-love. Doing the little things like affirming you are love, you are loving, and you are loved. Taking yourself out on an adventure. Going on a nature hike. Reading your favorite book. Sleeping in. Taking time off work. Doing a few of your favorite things every day. Know that you are worth it; how can you expect the world to change if it has nothing worth changing for? I take a note from Gandhi, "to be the change you seek in the world." You must realize you are worth it, and that you are the love you want to see in the world.

Keep this in mind every day. Affirm it to yourself. Be yourself. Then, the immediate world around you will change. Smile at others, make others feel how you feel for yourself. Then, they will start to want to do the same.

Be that gentle reminder that not all is doom and gloom by living and acting out of your very essence of love in your everyday interactions. They will start to change, and they will spread their love as well by just being their very essence that you reminded them of.

Once we reach a critical mass of love vibration, there will be no reason to want to fight or let people starve. Greed is the absence of love. Love is eternal, and infinitely abundant, for the core of you is also eternal and infinitely abundant (just look around you! There is so much to see and do!) So, if we all live our essence of love, then there will be no more greed, for we are already happy and fulfilled as realized beings of ardor.

The theme of the week was patience, so I will speak on that as well and relate it to self-love. The process of self-love is easy to understand, but in practice it can be difficult for some.

There will be others who will try to dissuade you from your path. Listen to them, for they are offering you a great lesson. Have patience with them. Retain your power. Arguments and negativity will only take you further from self-love. Listen to what they must say but detach from what they are saying. Never follow the path of another.

Ask yourself, "Is what they are saying going to increase the self-love I have for myself?" If the answer is no, then thank them for their guidance and continue following your path. If the answer is yes, then thank them for their guidance and continue following your path. You thank them either way, as an exercise in gratitude for every interaction is an opportunity to spread the love and to remind you of your essence of self-love.

It takes great patience to develop this skill, but do not fret. It takes time to master anything in this life! Patience, gratitude, and self-love. Simple concepts, divine results. Work hard at loving yourself and see what happens ...

Be love and be loved!

There you have it! Another energy reiterating that the essence of self-love can lead to all that we desire. We are advised to explore loving the you in you. The message is the same, just presented differently. Take time to let your hair down and enjoy the loving qualities that are uniquely you. To love the 'you' in you.

The young people's path is not so different than my own or most of the seekers who join me in the practice of spirituality. We all came to the place of wanting to know more and the desire to understand the topics we questioned in this lifetime. I bring this information to the forefront for two reasons. One, the story of these young people is extremely different than my own and, yet we have still crossed paths. Two, they are souls I would have never respected had I stayed in the confined box of my life before mysticism.

I am joining with the other forces of the Universe who bring this message to the masses. Let's move forward and make this love of self a reality in our own lives and the lives of those who wish to be a part of this loving energy. There is no fear, no damnation, and no money to be tithed. Just a willingness to let go of your past of a life filled with judgment and reach out to others who are ready to move forward on their path in this lifetime.

Taking classes filled with the enthusiasm and energy of others is my favorite way to learn. The interaction is priceless. Yes, teachers charge you to take these classes. They do so because they are giving up their precious time, compiling class materials and providing a service you want to share in. Also, there is an exchange of energy within the payment itself. In the past, I have found that if you give things away, there isn't a great deal of respect for the teaching or the assistance. If one must pay for something, there is more of a tendency to nurture and retain what you are being shown. It is up to you to discover which classes resonate with you and which ones do not. There is no reason to ever take a class if you don't feel that is a direction you wish to take. There are plenty of books to read, free at a library or on the internet as videos.

As always, dig as deeply as you can to be sure what material resonates and what does not. Not every modality is a fit for every soul, and there is only so much you will wish to absorb.

You will take with you whatever it is that your soul is seeking in this lifetime and tuck it into your tool box.

In my quest to think and love outside of my box, last summer I accepted an invitation to speak at the *Love Long Beach Festival*. Not really knowing the woman who had invited me and not knowing what to expect, I packed up a couple dozen books, my pen and bottled water. I arrived about thirty minutes early for my talk which is just part of who I am/was. The box, remember?

There I was, under their canopy, listening to the speaker before me. His talk was on the Chakra System. Interesting I thought, I will listen to this instead of wandering the beach.

As this young man moved further into his dialog, he began to explain how the right use of clearing your chakras with your partner leads to better sex. His personal story of how to attain the best sex of his life landed on my ears. Oh, my goodness! What was I doing here? My box was being shattered into millions of pieces by the words he was using, and I stood there in debate with myself. Should I go or stay?

Needing to take a minute, I moved out of the energy of the young man so that I could no longer hear his rhetoric. Breathe, I told myself. Breathe deeply and slowly and relax. I then heard, "It's your turn." I smiled at the young woman with tattoos running up her arms. It was too late to run.

Tentatively, I sat down on their blanket in the sand and began my talk. It was totally off the cuff with no preparation, just the knowledge that I would be talking to a small group of people and channeling Amadeus. Trusting my instincts, I began. My opening line was, "Just so you know, I will not be discussing sex. I am a 66-year-old woman who keeps some things private. Sex is one of those things." This brought about howling laughter. I had captured my audience. I proceeded and began to channel Amadeus.

The message from the Other Side was clear. Learn to love yourself. Respect who you are. I then proceeded to tell them how ten years prior to our meeting I would have never accepted such a crazy invitation as I had that weekend. I spoke boldly, "Look at your tattoos, your hair is pink, and you, you have drawn a clown's mouth on your face." They looked at me in silence. I then continued, "I am different these days and I accept you for the beautiful energy you are projecting and respect your right to be you."

"I do wish to speak of the homeless. I want to invite you to know them. They, too, have loving energy, but have fallen on hard times or have an illness that takes them out of anyone's box. Please, when you pass a displaced person, give them a smile. They don't always want a donation as they are cared for by many. Yet, they almost never have someone say hello and smile. I implore you to change their life and yours by this simple act."

The talk continued for my allotted forty-five minutes with a wonderful question and answer period. There was much laughter and giggling during my presentation on the beach that day and a round of applause as I finished. The conversations with the audience afterwards suggested I had made a difference in their thought process. They were all about love and peace but hadn't thought about the kindness they could bring to others they normally ignored. I felt so at home with these young people. Where was my box? I left it in the trunk of my car, so I could leave judgment behind.

Oh, the growth I have embedded into my soul in this lifetime! I see the love of me pouring out and teaching others. I thank those on the Other Side for bringing the gift of love of self and forgiveness for my birth family for the chaos we endured together.

Greetings, Sweet One. It is I, Amadeus.

Yes, your box is shifting and changing as you continue your path in the spiritual realm. You are so much more engaging as you accept the differences of others on your path. They too have a story and you do not know what that may be unless they choose to share it.

The amount of time you were sitting tightly in your box of judgment was lengthy. It has taken a while to help you to break down the sides of the box, yet you are doing it with grace and purpose.

You have come to realize that you are meeting so many more interesting people with the paper bag you have created recently to replace the rigid box. We love it when you laugh and tell others one day you will just be in no bag at all. We love the amusement you have taken in realizing that you were in a box and that as you shift and change and accept more differences in the world, you will find no need for any restraints on you.

As we love you, we also love the growth you have experienced and the fact that you know you are ever-evolving with more to learn and with more growth to accomplish. Keep moving

forward and shining your light as you are using yourself as an example for others to overcome their boxes and step out of judgment.
Go this day in Truth and Happiness.

Loving you as you are, Amadeus.

CHAPTER XX

Realities of the Child

s I begin this new chapter, I must remember to close my eyes and type while listening for the messages to be brought in today. The weekend was filled with family love. The youngest grandchild turned one. His party was a superb success as he was given a cake of his own to smash into and he did just that, with one-year-old glee.

The wide-eyed wonder of this boy only knew those he recognized at his house that day. The others were strangers who had come to celebrate with his mom and dad. He was entertained by them and by the gifts they had brought. He did not even know it was his birthday.

Here is the time in his life when he will begin to find out that there is such a preoccupation with rules to live by. For society and for his safety. The little girl, who is three, played at his water table. He wanted the things she had and reached out for them. "No," she said. "I am playing with these, find something else." Had he just heard that? What does it mean? This is my new water table and I want my toys!

Yes, this is where and how it begins. This is when the child learns that the world is not his alone and that he must learn how to share. He does not want to share. He has never heard of that concept.

Inside his home, locks have been installed on all the kitchen cabinets, so he cannot get to his favorite pots and pans. Quizzically, he fights with the door, alas he cannot open it! For now, mommy picks him up and takes him back to his toys.

Then, there is the gate that blocks him from leaving the family room and kitchen. It is meant for his safety, so he cannot climb the stairs and fall. Yet, others can go through the gate and move about easily. He is not questioning that contraption yet, as he doesn't understand the concept. All he knows is that he can stand up and lean on it but can't get through it to play with the kitties. The kitties are happy about that!

These are little things, but when you are only one-year old, you don't have much to compare it to. Soon, more rules will fall into place. The word "no" will become a big part of his world. His parents are gentle and loving. It won't take long for him to find out that not everyone is so gentle. There will be the boy who pushes him out of the swing. He won't know what is going on in his normally safe world. Then, he will snatch a toy from another and he will get either walloped by the other child or disciplined by others and not understand. This little guy is on his way to being put in a box.

Mom and dad will continue to love him but will provide him with the necessary rules to help him adjust to society. They will be proud of him when he does good things. Yet, they will be disciplinarians when necessary.

Preschool will have a new set of rules to follow. Then, first grade and beyond.

More rules will follow with each passing day as this boy grows and flourishes. Some of the rules will make sense, and some won't. Sometimes action will be taken to make him fit into the box that has been created for him, or he will wiggle outside of the box and remain in constant discipline.

This is how we begin to question love of self. How can it be? If I was born perfect, then what are all these rules and corrections? Why is the word 'no' used so often?

Soon, I will be playing the 'I love me' game. I will also share this book with this beautiful addition to my family and soul group. Through games and play, I will teach him to love everything about himself. I hope to teach his parents how to play it, so they can enjoy the game with him. This is the game I want you to play with yourself.

There are so many children in the world who will not be invited to play this fun game as there will be no one nearby who knows this is what they should be teaching and playing. With the power I am being granted, I will be asking you to play this game, and to play it with all the children you meet. We must take it to the schools and have it become part of the curriculum. Preschools, day-cares, private home care facilities. Kindergarten is one of the dearest places to teach this game. As the children learn more about the box, let's teach them about learning to love themselves also! Then they will not even accept a paper bag!

If you could touch five children and those five children could touch another five children with this game, can you visualize the ball rolling out into the streets of your town? Why shouldn't it? The only thing stopping it from progressing is you and me. It is up to us to pick up the movement and release it to the public. You might be the one to write a catchy jingle that is fun for the children to listen to while they play this game. It is inevitable that, with your excitement, we can create an avalanche of loving beings right before our very eyes. I will explain this game more fully in the following chapter.

I cannot undertake this massive task alone. My intention is not to bask in the glory of what might come. Rather, I seek nothing but to teach the concept of loving oneself. I am asking that we team up to accomplish the mission at hand. We can make this a phenomenal group effort that will change the Earth, as we know it. Forever. Yes, some will ridicule the concept that this could change the vibration of the world and we will let them think their thoughts. Should you choose to believe them, that is your right. But, if you don't, think of the good it might do for the world. There is no harm in this game, only goodness and love.

I hear many people talk about this same subject and have read many books referring to the mirror technique. This is me, asking you to join in the celebration of the perfection of you. If you have not yet learned to love yourself passionately, then why not learn alongside the children? They don't need to be aware you are also learning if you do not want them to know. Or, you can be totally forthright and inform them that by watching them loving themselves you are also learning to love yourself.

Be brave, Dear Ones. Step into this new light and own its power of illumination of all souls. There is no better time than the present. Don't you agree?

It is I, Amadeus. Greetings, Dear One, on this glorious day.

You sit there in your favorite chair, looking out the window with the breeze moving the roses and tree leaves, and the wind chime softly playing a song for you. It is your favorite place in the entire home.

You are remembering the loving weekend that just passed as you saw your boys and their wives, their parents and siblings and the little babies.

You are developing the gift of self-love as you introduce the concept. Some of the relatives are interested and some are not. The discussions with the women of the family were deep and revealing. You have shared stories that you hadn't spoken of before. This is part of the forgiveness and letting go of guilt in a situation you had no control over.

Damon has asked that you let go of the guilt of a private matter in the family. It took the events of this weekend for you to realize that you were still holding onto it. We are so proud of you! You took this step, after finally recognizing what issue he was referring to.

Another petal of the rose has been peeled back and now the rose hip of fragrance is your reward. Keep working on the self-love, Dear

One, always coming back to center. Loving the 'you' in you.

You are beautiful, loving and supportive of your family, and it is time to behave the same way with you, Frances, the name you chose to carry in this current lifetime.

Understand the impact of asking others to join in your passion instead of pretending you are in this alone. You are surrounded by many who love you on the earth plane, not just here on the Other Side. Go in love and light this day and bring joy to the world.

Love, Amadeus!

CHAPTER XXI

The Love of a Child Game

I would like to take time now to teach you about the love of the child. As we all know, the infant comes into the world with no verbiage of its own. But it does have a voice to be reckoned with. The little being speaks with the only language it knows. Wailing! And wail they will. We swaddle them, feed them, diaper them and cross our fingers that we might get some rest before the next cry for assistance. By doing this we are showing our unconditional love of them, if they belong to the group of lucky ones; those who are loved and not abused.

They do not know, at the very beginning of life on Earth, that this caring attention is how we show our affection for them. All they know is they are no longer frightened, hungry or uncomfortable. They know the sound of the voices who were around when the babe was still in utero, but the beings they belong to are just shadows to them for some time as their eyesight develops. They recognize the energy of those who are caring for them.

At last, the day comes when they can see our faces and smile when they hear our voices! They are Divine perfection. They have come into the world without any preconceived notions of how it will be. These small creatures merely exist. In that existence, they are the most beautiful mortals we can put our eyes on. We count their fingers and their toes to assure ourselves all is right in the world. We know not what they have brought with them from past lives or from their current visit to the Other Side. If only they could speak at this young age and tell all they know or remember.

Should our newborn not be in a perfect body or in perfect health, they are loved with the same abandon as any other infant. Because, they chose you and you chose them a long time ago, before you were born, and you open your heart and fill it with their essence. They will have their own lessons to learn, but we know not what those experiences are at this point.

As the child grows, a miniature box is built, as I said before. They are taught how to have good manners and to not bite or hit. All good things, but for a toddler who is born knowing they are perfect, they get confused about the confines of this crate. They test their parents or guardians. They want to be loved, but they are trying to assert their own personalities into the world. Sometimes, they just don't fit right. The box may be too tight or too loose. They push the parameters to see how far they can go.

We must be reminded that the child has a soul of its own. They are there for you to parent, not create them as your image.

Just because I wanted to be a physical education teacher and it was outside of the realms of possibility, does not mean any of my children wished to be a teacher. None of them did.

Not a single child of mine was interested in any of the things that I would have loved to pursue in my childhood. They are individuals and even though I did not realize I was practicing good parenting by not forcing my passions on them, I was. I was allowing each one of them to grow. I watered, fertilized them and put them in the sun. They developed into unique individuals with their own personal journeys. Hopefully I let their box become invisible ... not even a bag.

As infants, it is extremely important that we teach them to love themselves as they did the moment they were born. The next paragraph describes a fun game parents and children can play together. It helps with one of the most important tasks in parenting. I had never heard of this concept. The adage applies here; I wish I knew then what I know now, but none of us were born with directions to the parent written on our bottoms!

Stand the child in front of a mirror as soon as they can grasp the concept that the child in the mirror is really them. Have them touch their hair, their eyes, their nose, their mouth, etc. As you do this, continually repeat their love of each. I love the color of my hair, I love my curly hair, my straight hair. I love the color of my eyes, the size of my nose, and the shape of my lips. Giggle with them and cuddle. Have them love the color of their skin, their family history and their family's religion (We know as they grow and question life, they may change their religious beliefs, but as a little one we wish for them to honor what they are being taught.) We also wish for them to appreciate their sexuality, but at the young age of three or four, they may not question this subject. As they grow and learn, they can more readily accept differences in themselves as they already love who they are. They are to love this child in the mirror, exactly as they are.

Let them feel the love of themselves. Love each part of the entire body! There will come a time when this is no longer their favorite game but consider now the self-esteem you have given them. And think about what it has done for you as you played alongside of them. This is a game, but a very serious one indeed.

You have not taught them that they are entitled to all that they wish for in the world. You have taught them of their perfection and their love of self which will help them climb the mountains of success that they may wish for in this lifetime.

The second part of this game is for you! You touch your hair, eyes, nose and mouth! You love those pieces of you alongside your child. This gives you a leg up to those who don't have little ones to teach it to but must stand in front of their own mirror alone and learn of this love. I had to begin in front of my bathroom mirror as my children were grown when I learned of this game but will now play it with my grandchildren and others and watch them grow.

This respect of themselves is not boastful or braggart. It is an innate knowing that throughout life they can know of this well-loved feeling and will not have to learn it as an adult. It is an integral part of self that engrains the concept of love that emanates to others.

From this very notion of love of self, the energy field of the soul brings the sensation of love to whomever comes near. The person nearing this love field of this child may not even realize that they are feeling kinder and more lighthearted, yet this is what will happen.

From infant to preschooler, these children develop and grow. They enter kindergarten and the teacher tells them they cannot color outside of the lines. They are shown how to print their letters and to read words. The box is getting bigger and there are more rules such as no running in the hallways, raise your hand to speak, etc. Imagine the private child having to raise his hand and ask to go to the bathroom. Some are so taken aback by this seemingly simple task that they soil themselves to avoid attention. And now they stand in the limelight being ushered out of the room in front of everyone! This is so wrong on so many levels, but society is asking for rules and the rules are being taught.

(Yes, I do know there must be some things that help the child function in society in harmony, but these lessons need to be taught with loving understanding of the whole child. Yes, the classroom is a difficult place to achieve what I am proposing, yet if the child has been playing this game throughout its young lifetime they will succeed no matter what.)

Now the little one is wondering why they are always being corrected. They begin to wonder why, if they were born perfect, are they being disciplined so. The child begins to quietly and secretly wonder about this perfection, this love of themselves without being conscious of the thought. If you continue the 'love of self' game, they can come back to the place of bliss and know that the rules are just helping them to walk together in peace in society. You will teach them this tenet.

Amadeus has taught this game to me and I will play it with as many children as I am able. He has instructed me to get this message into the world. He has told me that when these children are reminded to love themselves in this way, this love will emanate from their very beings and will spread to others. Amadeus has said, "There can be peace in the world and starvation and hopelessness will fade away." This may not happen in my lifetime, but I'm elated to know it has begun and can be built upon until all wars cease and humanity lives in the light of love.

So, what would happen if you gave this game a try? Do you foretell anything unhealthy in this practice? I get a feeling of elation thinking of more and more parents, all over the world teaching what Amadeus has taught me. I know I have repeated this message more than once, but that is the theme of this book. This is what I am to teach, and I feel that repetition of an idea is a good teaching tool.

Amadeus has said, teach it to the children. At one point during a meditation, it dawned on me that we are all God's children, so let's teach it to all of us! It will pick up power and speed as it races through the masses. Teach it in the prisons, halfway houses, rehabilitation centers. Teach, teach, and teach. Love yourself in a way you never considered before. Love the body you are in and take care of it! Love every miniscule part of your being.

It is I, Amadeus.

You have built upon the words I taught to you and you have done well with your story. These children who learn this and teach it to others will resonate with love of self and that love will spread throughout the world and history. It is from this very small step that world peace,

elimination of poverty and of hunger will reign upon the Earth.

You, Dear One, are taking this message on the road to be played throughout the days and evenings going forward. People will listen. They may not believe the outcome can really be achieved as I have laid it out before you, but it is Truth. This will not happen overnight, but it will happen. It is a mammoth task we have asked you to undertake. We would not have asked this of you if we did not think you capable.

You are strong and determined and unequivocally able to bring this message to the others as you have been guided to do. You may not be alive on the Earth to see its success, but you will see it from the Other Side. Know the enormity of this and continue to go in peace this day.

Love, Amadeus

CHAPTER XXII

Addressing Depression

A s I am about to bring this missive to a close, I wish to address the recent suicides being reported more frequently in the news the past few years, from children to elders. There is a constant feeling of not being good enough. Not being smart enough. Not being athletic enough. Some are just being bullied to a point where they do not see happiness in front of them. There is not enough love of self.

Depression needs to find its way out of the closet. It clearly needs to become something we are able to talk to with our parents, teachers, clergy and peers. I don't claim to be an expert on this subject, but feel that love of self enters into some of this equation. There are definitely medications that must be included in this diagnosis as the chemicals in the brain are just not functioning properly in many instances. Yet, at times, there are just certain situations which are difficult to handle, and despair sets in for periods of time, not for the entire lifetime.

Just today, I had a friend come out on social media to talk about her depression and look for answers and to ask others to speak out. A month ago, after the recent celebrity suicides, a friend of my son, Damon, spoke of her depression and how she can't describe it to others and how she is so alone. We need more work done in this area. We are in crisis with lack of love of self and lack of the ability to overcome despair.

When in deep depression, nothing matters. The escape is the answer for the soul. There is no one who can penetrate. We need to begin conversations about depression, so we can actually penetrate to the soul level. I will try. I hope I will succeed. I pray and will be guides by God and Spirit.

How can love of self help to overcome the occasional bouts of hopelessness that envelope one at any given time? If one is in a state of loving themselves, it becomes easier to recognize a down time and bring the soul back into happiness quicker. Should one be in a clinical state of melancholy, love of self, combined with proper diet, exercise and medication, if needed, would work together to bring balance to the soul.

I know that many schools and educators are trying to find a solution to the bullying that is going on with children as it has since the beginning of time, perhaps. Social media has heightened the awareness of those being made fun of and made them more reclusive and inclined to end their lives. If they had been taught love of self, I believe they would have more confidence to overcome that which is being thrown at them by others. Believing in loving the 'you' in you should become the norm, not the exception. The bully himself could benefit from being taught to love himself so that there was no angst that might bring them to feel insecure and make fun of another person in the first place.

I am bringing this to life in this book to introduce a few new thoughts regarding love of self. Why shouldn't we invest time in a simple game of looking in the mirror to bring about a change in the lives of so many who walk the Earth? Yes, I call it simple, but it is extremely difficult and involved. For adults, it's not a silly game to love your body parts and your personality. It is deeper. It is hard work to overcome the atrocities done to our souls in childhood. Can we catch the children before these horrific things can attack their little bodies and young souls? Only with open discussions and constant supervision of our babies.

We may not able to control all of the depression and subsequent suicide, but by bringing it to the forefront, we will enable many to openly discuss their feelings and proceed to seek help from others to control some of the loneliness they feel. When I did not feel I loved me, I too fell into days where I thought I was alone in the world. By changing the pattern, I was able to change the thoughts and smile in gratitude for each day. That is what I wish for everyone. Yes, this is a big dream. Yes, it needs to start now. Each day is precious, and none should be wasted. The sooner we can get this information into everyone's hands, the sooner we can slow this epidemic.

Realizing that one cannot reveal exactly what it is that is causing their unhappiness they should be allowed to talk about it the best way they know how. We must listen. We must not ignore the signs that someone is no longer communicating in the ways they had been. Being closed in a room instead of mingling with the family is a definite sign that some sort of loving conversation should be taking place. Not showing up for events should bring notice that something may not be right with a friend or family member. Choose to pay attention to all signs in your friends, co-workers or family that there has been a change in behavior. All we can do is our best. If someone is really ready to take their life and nothing we do changes that, do not feel guilty as you are only able to assist someone who is open to that assistance.

With the onslaught of social media, television and movies, the young people are more aware of what they don't have. They feel they are not as beautiful, gifted, educated or rich as others. They fall into a downward spiral. Depression ensues and the idea that the world would be better off without them or that their personal pain is agonizing brings about death and pain to all who loved them. There is too much anger in the world. It is our job, our commitment to the children and others to bring love of self to their worlds so they see their worth and they talk about their depression so that we can end the madness.

Now that I have brought this out of the closet and onto the table where it belongs, let's see what we can do to teach love of self to the children and all souls who are ready to accept that concept. I will leave the therapists to do their work, but I will not stop asking for all to love themselves freely and with abandon. Let's work together to make a change in the world.

Love the 'you' in you as I love the 'me' in me. Sending blessings for a love filled life from this day forward.

It is Justine, Loving One

It is with wonder and joy that we follow you as you write of depression and some of the reasons

for the current upswing in suicide. We love the way you address it and make sure everyone knows that they can suggest help but are not to take on the energy of guilt if their loved one chooses death instead of help from medical professionals. Your heart is so full of love when you discuss this. There will be more of this subject in another book.

Sending love this day, Justine

CHAPTER XXIII

Others Are Teaching of Love

To have known, when my children were babies, all that I know now! They are remarkable being, despite my shortcomings in teaching them as was pointed out by my daughter in her forward message in the front of this book. To know then what I know now is recognized by me, but I do not beat myself up in any way. I am on the journey I chose for me and they are on the individual paths they chose for themselves. I see an easier vision for child-rearing for others in this lifetime due to the spiritual awakening of so many parents. I am instructed to help to teach the innocence of the newborn soul to all who will listen and to help bring love of self to children.

We, the children of the Universe, are perfect beings. Still, we choose to openly compete with the energy of others. We choose to live our life's shortcomings through our children, trying to give them what we did not have in our own lives. As you will remember, I was not raised with hugs and kisses. I taught myself to embrace that behavior and began to shower it upon my own family, and anyone else who would allow my energy into theirs.

So, it is that I have been introduced, via paperback or electronic device, to the world of others speaking the same truth that I am bringing to you in this manuscript. The message flows from the mind out of the tips of my fingers as they continue their waltz across the leaves of this book. It is one that is filled with undying love for the beauty of the Earth to become free of the wars which plague its very essence. Yes, there have been wars for untold centuries and they are not isolated, but currently being waged around the world.

This energy takes me to a song that resonated passionately with me in my teen years. It may have been that I always knew this was my agreement but had just forgotten it until it was introduced to me through Amadeus. Perhaps you remember it, perhaps you have never heard it, but the words clearly bounce through my mind as if it were only yesterday. "Let there be peace on Earth and let it begin with me."

Sy Miller and Jill Jackson wrote this song, the lyrics about their dream of world peace, "Let There Be Peace on Earth." They believed we could co-create this energy. I have revived this memory as a synchronicity as I continue to agree with them.

Here I am, decades later, singing these lyrics with no restraint and believing it is a possibility. And, that I could be a catalyst in birthing the concept that world peace can and will become a reality. Who says it cannot be in my lifetime? I accept no negative energy with this dream. It is possible. If it takes future generations, so be it. It must be fueled by the energy of this generation. We must act. I no longer wish to hide in the shadows hoping others will heed my request for peace.

I must admit, after watching Dr. Shefali, a world-renowned clinical psychologist who received her doctorate from Columbia University, New York, on Super Soul Sunday and hearing her speak with Oprah Winfrey, I began to feel slightly insecure about who I am and how I think I can change the world. I wallowed in that vibration for a while and spoke to others about how amazing she was. I was ignoring my own love of self and erroneously began comparing myself to another lovely being.

By the following Sunday, when I turned on the show again, I had returned to my self-love regarding speaking in public. We are all perfect in the body, voice, education and the particular energy we have chosen for our current journey. I must remember to practice what I preach. I am back on target and ready to bring my voice to the public sector.

Dr. Shefali, I firmly believe, is the individual I was encouraged to find by Amadeus in the previous chapter.

It is I, Amadeus. Greetings this day, Dear One.

You are relaxing and writing and putting all other thoughts at bay. The classical music you are playing is helping to sooth your soul.

Thank you for trusting the message last night. We know you needed to speak to your

husband but were delighted you called on us to make certain of his safety. (My husband was on a trip without me and I had not heard from him by 11 p.m. his time. I needed comfort that my concerns were in vain and yes, they were. Soon thereafter, we were able to make connections and I heard the joy of his journey to his destination.)

Know Kalai, a dear contact of yours, is on this journey to assist you. You know she holds a special energy with you. She was set purposefully on your path to bring you to a point where you trust yourself and know that you are going to be courageous and well received. We mention her here as she will be accompanying you many places and be filled with reminding you of your love of you.

Yesterday, we heard self-doubt as you listened to this highly educated woman speak, Dr. Shefali. You allowed a lack of formal education to interfere with your energy, albeit for a while. You sat in that 'lesser than' energy for some time until you pulled yourself out and reassured yourself that you too will be heard. You are critical to the masses. So many are similar to you in their self-judgment. You slipped, but you righted yourself and moved back into the energy of 'I need to do this'. This is my purpose; I do love the 'me in me'. No amount of education can compete with a soul's purpose. You have your purpose as Dr. Shefali has her own.

There may never be an original idea (as you were taught in design school), but there is a collective of energy working together to bring about the consciousness that is needed to propel the world into peace.

There can only be a coming together of minds to speak the message in the thoughts that are going to resonate with each individual soul on the level they are working on at any given moment. Go, therefore, and greet your audience with aplomb and pure delight. You have the ability to bring lightness to a very dramatic situation.

As we have spoken with you before, there are forces to be reckoned with and it is time to fortify humans to protect themselves from the energy of these radical groups. Some are more inhumane than others, but all will stop at nothing to gain control and to erase those energies they do not wish to resonate with. Had they been taught love of self, they would also see that every life has purpose and is unquestionably needed for the Earth to ebb and flow as was intended.

Recognize, Dear One, that if this ill will had not found its way to the planet, your message would not be as critical as it is because all would already be living in the love energy. This is not meant to justify their being here, but only to allow you to realize the importance of your work. This is the work you have been sent to

do in this lifetime. It will not exist in lifetimes to come as the planet will be healed. In another incarnation, you will have another purpose. And so, it is.

Love, Amadeus

CHAPTER XXIV

Angels Healing Hearts

"And so, it is," they say. And so, it is. I began playing around with a logo quite a few years ago and came up with *Angels Healing Hearts*. It seemed clear to me that was to be my message and that was what I was here to do. This is what I am doing by bringing this information to you.

I continue to talk about looking at yourself in the mirror and learning to love yourself, but the actual message is somehow not as powerful as when I remind you to use your Angels to help heal the pain of what was, so we can move you to where you want to be. Some of us have been shaken to our core. My chaos does not begin to compare with the chaos of others' lives. I didn't suffer sexual abuse, being burned with cigarettes or the atrocities of starving each day. These things and others take much more work than I had to do. It can take a lifetime to work through feeling loved and being enough. Let's just see if we can move it along with what I call a game. It is definitely not a game to some, but a means of survival.

Each of us have multitudes of Angels with us. We have Arch-Angels, Ascended Masters, and Guardian Angels and so on. The Angels often feel lonely as we forget they are there and that they are there to assist us. There is not one request too big or too small for them to assist and solve. Why not call on the Angels who sit with you always?

As I continued to grow in my self-confidence of knowing what was happening in another's life energy field and being able to bring forth messages from the dearly departed, I found myself in need of a business card that was not so ordinary; not one from the discounters. If any of you are aware of the many budget printers, they have numerous samples of cards, you select the one you want, type in your information and for a nominal sum you are ready to receive your cards in the mail.

I enlisted the artistic help of a kind man with a ready smile, Dennis Nozawa. He is a medium and quite gifted. He draws a picture of the person he is connecting with and writes their message on the picture. He continues the reading, all the while sketching and receiving information. He and I became friends, and his easy demeanor was always there for me at faires or classes. He is also a graphic designer. Lucky for me.

When I was ready for that permanent artwork, this mild-mannered man was a stress-free decision. He was comfortable to work with. Within a few short weeks, we had the final image. You will see it on my website, francespullin.com. Often, I silently thank him as I hand over another beautiful card.

At times, we change the information on the card, but the logo remains solid and true.

I need to get back to healing hearts. At times, in one of my classes, someone has a breakthrough and is touched to the point of tears! It is in that moment I know I am on the right path. As my students continue to show up, their emotional traumas continue to be healed. If we do not finish the session during class, I am a moment away by phone.

There is so much work to be done, I will be doing webinars and seminars teaching self-love. I will create events in other states in other metaphysical venues. I plan to attract more and more seekers as they learn about my message and my intent to help them. I move forward every day to that end. I hope to connect with you one day and assist you with healing whatever it is you need to heal in order to get to that warm place of self-love. And, I will be teaching others to teach what I teach. To give them a script so we can connect with the multitudes.

Private sessions, which produce so much recovery, will become my new norm. I will have my own office and clear the energy according to how I have been taught. The schedule will be kept neatly in line and the door will be open to those the Universe sends. I am ready, willing, and able to accept my life's purpose and be supported by my Team as we endeavor to heal all who enter my energy.

I will continue to channel Amadeus and his messages. They come from a wizened old soul who has survived many lifetimes on the Earth, and in other realms, to bring himself through me to the masses. He continues to broadcast his message of loving oneself. Amadeus is a master of teaching and promoting the love of self-concept! He believes in it with conviction and has taught me to follow his lead.

I will bring the soul of each person that I work with forward and we will talk with their Angels and Guides, and the rest of their Team. I will teach them how easy it is to get in touch with their Angels at any given moment. You must be in gratitude for all you are being given at any time and space in this lifetime and in those to come.

Some beings are able to clearly see the Angels who dance around us and whisper in our ears. I have not had that blessing yet, but one never knows what untold miracles the next day may have in store. I am more of a "knower" than a "seer" and so I am content with the gift given unto me. At times, I have seen the quick light of the Fairy as it danced around the room, but the Angels have made their presence known to me only in their own all-knowing ways. I am in gratitude of my gifts.

If we are always surrounded with so much love, why do we not live in complete selflessness, complete love? The answer is quite simple. We do not remember they are with us and we do not remember to ask for the help we are seeking. Most of us have forgotten that we brought them with us into this lifetime. As infants, we knew and then we did not.

It would be easy to have a more blissful life if we could get into the habit of bringing in our Angels into every situation that we face. Why not ask them for green lights when you are running late? Small, senseless you may feel, but what if it works and you arrive within five minutes of the appointed time? What then? What and how would you feel? Would you feel simple gratitude?

Start practicing ... ask for something simple. Something that is easy for them to fulfill, but that would really amaze you. That will be the beginning of you trusting that they are there for you even for the simplest things to solve. Ask for an open table at a popular restaurant on a Friday night without a reservation. See if that one table just had a cancellation. Yes, take notice each time you ask and each time they provide you with the gift you requested. Thank them, always.

Angels, Angels, Angels ... they are everywhere, filled with giggles, laughter and mirth yet they are serious when they need to be. You can never go wrong when you ask your Angels to step in and work with you.

My own experience with Angels has been remarkable. One time, I met one of my Angels at a car accident that was my fault. He was dressed as a policeman and was directing traffic, or so I thought. He smiled at me, and I felt pretty and flirtatious in his presence. I actually felt the power of his love around me. This was uncharacteristic behavior for me, as I am almost fearful of the magnificent power of police officers.

As children, we were taught to respect them like no other. Once when my older sister was a teenager and strutting her stuff, she was out on the lawn and talking to us about the 'cops'. My mother overheard the conversation and my sister was loudly admonished. She stated emphatically that they were 'police officers' and that she never wanted to hear them disrespected again.

As the gorgeous, young officer directed me that day, I turned into oncoming traffic and was slammed by the biggest, reddest, newest Suburban I had ever seen! You may sit in amazement while you read this and wonder why my Angel would have set up a car wreck. You see, I had a car accident in my energy. I knew this. I had verbalized it to my boys as I drove them to school that morning. I asked them to please keep me calm so that I would not hurt anyone; especially the children. Heavy traffic at the school caused undue aggravation for me as I waited for mothers to drop off their children. I watched them thoughtlessly pull into the first spot, drop off their children and wait for kisses goodbye. All the while, the remainder of us waited and watched the performance that was tying up a massive gaggle of traffic. It irritated me that they were not thoughtful of the rest of the cars stacking up behind them in the street. As you see, I was still in my box.

You wonder why the Angel could not stop the accident from happening, I'm sure. I had made this a part of my contract before being born so that I could feel the energy of the Angels who loved me and be convinced of their power.

This occurred at a time before my son crossed over and, back then, I had no idea what a spiritual journey was. I was like many of you and most of the world. Rushed, annoyed, thinking these drivers only in their thoughts when I was only in mine. It is not the time of my life I am most proud of. I have forgiven me for the tension I was creating in the Universe. I have made unbelievable changes since then.

As I entered the intersection that morning, where an earlier car accident was being cleared, my Angel appeared as the police man, and directed me into a 'safe' accident situation where no one was injured. Two cars were totaled. Both drivers walked away from the scene and caught a ride home, while our vehicles were hauled onto flatbeds and taken to their respective repair facilities. Well, his went to be repaired and mine went to the destroyed car boneyard to be sold for parts.

In every car accident, I have experienced in this lifetime, I have walked away virtually unscathed. I was seventeen when my girlfriend, driving her Renault, was hit by a big Cadillac. We were told the Renault flipped three times. I awoke on the back seat of the car and crawled out. An officer walked me to the police car and placed me in the rear seat as we waited for the ambulance. (Did you know there are no door handles in the back seat of a patrol car? In my shock, that struck me as more frightening than the accident itself. Claustrophobia set in, and I sat fearfully awaiting my escape.) Neither of us had even a broken fingernail! Angels saved us for sure!

Imagine the Angels surrounding you in every heartfelt moment. They were there at your birth. They walked with you through all of the crises on your journey. They protected you to the extent that you invited them to, or that you had agreed to before reincarnating for this lifetime. They will also be with you as you draw your last breath and escort you to the Other Side.

Were they there when the belt flew in my childhood home? You bet. One morning before school, the belt was yanked from its loops, folded in half and swung toward me. My father's grip was loose, the actual buckle slid across my face. Yet, with all the force that had been rendered behind the swing, it missed my right eye by an inch. I must have made an agreement that I would not go through life without sight in one eye. My Angels stood erect and the eye was safe, and the discipline ended with my father's remorse. He did not ever mean to harm, only to teach.

My belief in the power of Angels can never be argued. I will tell my stories, close my lips and no confrontation can be pursued. No one, no one, can force me to deny the presence of the love and protection that angels have brought into my life. Now that I believe in them, there is no way to shake my determination of their existence.

Go now. Call on them. Ask them to simply get you safely to sleep if you are reading this before you sleep. Ask them to watch over your drive to work and make your arrival on time and without incident on the road. Ask them to give you a sign that they are with you. And now, listen. I hear their feather's ruffling as they enter the scene.

> *It is Jerod this day, Dear One. Your Guardian Angel has come to speak.*
>
> *You have so beautifully described your belief in Angels. We so appreciate that you have written of us and confirmed that you and I have met, and that your belief is strong. It is so apparent, as you write, that you felt the love I was sending to you to protect you as you pulled into the inevitable accident. Yes, I sent you into that space, but not without the protection you needed to walk away from the scene and fetch a ride home with that lovely woman who was your client as well as your friend.*
>
> *Angels are numerous. Very few have ever walked the Earth, but there are a few. I am not one of them. I have always resided on the Other Side and I have watched over many of you humans for eons and eons. I do not recall when I was not here. I do not recall the day I began my work. One day, I was here. I had charges on the Earth that I was instructed to listen to and assist when they called or when they needed me.*

I have loved the 'position' I have been given as I work to keep so many safe and on their safest path. I remember nothing else. I was created to do this work and to not falter. Giving love and receiving thanks for a job well done is all that is needed to send me on to the next loving occurrence I am called upon to facilitate.

Go in love this beautiful day and remember the love vibration you felt when we were together in the Earth's energy.

Love always and always, Jerod.

IN CONCLUSION

The last concept I wish to leave you with in this story is that I began my tale of life with the obscure notion that I was not loved by my parents. It has been within these pages that I came to realize they truly did love me. They loved me to the best of their ability. I took that love and changed it, rearranged it and created my own version of love which I thought was different for my own children. That is not to say I was the best at what I did, it's just that I love me, and I love the way I raised my flock.

I have recently learned Mother Mary is on of my Guides also. When I wrote with her, she said, "You are thinking that if I have always been with you, why did I allow the beatings? I must tell you, Beautiful One, without the lessons learned in childhood, this book could not have happened. Accept my love and know that when the belt landed beside your eye that early morning many years ago, it was I, along with Jerod your Guardian Angel, who saved it from hitting the eye directly. You have a lovely face without any evidence of the act bestowed on you by your father". So it is, that I write this book of love and healing of my soul.

I enjoy my growth and my gifts of teaching and healing. I am being applauded from the Other Side for learning what I have written here and engaging you, my audience, to join me in whatever beliefs you glean from its pages.

It is now that I wish to thank all who listened to me talk about this book for the past three years as I moved through the process of loving myself in a way that I could push aside self-recriminating thoughts and negative emotions. It has not been an easy journey as I took myself apart and examined who I was and who I wanted to become. I took time to forgive myself, my parents, exes including all who are no longer a part of my life, just a part of my story. It is a tale, you know. I saw things through my eyes and perhaps misconstrued them at times. All of that is behind me until I slip, fall, and right myself again. I do expect this to be the process of my life going forward, but it will be easier each day.

Standing in gratitude of the Energy Source/God for the life I have had this time on Earth. I have been allowed to grow and make changes to the 'Me in Me'. I have been able to help others with their journey and now I am publishing my second book to leave a legacy to my children and grandchildren when I leave the energy of Earth one more time.

Go in love, light and laughter for Eternity! Always, Frances

IN GRATITUDE

Gratitude goes to the following souls who assisted on my healing journey and who assisted in contributing something to this publication.

Kevin Pullin, my loving husband, who not wanting to, did the final edit and made me feel more secure in what I was sending you, my audience.

My parents, Warren and Esther for my journey blending with theirs when it was not so loving to now, when it is.

For my children for returning freely the love I gave to them.

To my editor, Roni Askey-Doran for her guidance.

To my friends, Christina Gikas, Elizabeth Bonzo-Savage, Lani Kay, Carolle Weels Vargas, Nancy Pilato for their review, feedback and editing processes after final review with my editor.

And to those who assisted on my spiritual path, Gabriel with his music, Rebecca with her channeling included in this missive, Christina for her guidance through hypnotherapy sessions, Kalai for just being there to hold space, and to others too numerous to mention, you stand in the light with me. I love you all!

I wish to thank my Guides, Angels, Elementals and my son, Damon. Thank you all for taking time to work with me and deliver this book to those who are awaiting its publication, so they may begin their journeys into self-love.

CPSIA information can be obtained
at www.ICGtesting.com
Printed in the USA
FSHW021746290519
58518FS